CHILDREN AT THE FRONT

A
DIFFERENT
VIEW
OF
THE
WAR
ON
ALCOHOL
AND
DRUGS

The CWLA North American Commission on
Chemical Dependency and Child Welfare
Final Report and Recommendations

Richard L. Jones, Commission Chair
Charlotte McCullough, Director, CWLA Chemical Dependency Initiative

CHILD WELFARE LEAGUE OF AMERICA
WASHINGTON, DC

Child Welfare League of America, Inc.
440 First Street, NW, Suite 310, Washington, DC 20001-2085

Current Printing (last digit)
10 9 8 7 6 5 4 3 2 1

Cover design by S. Dmitri Lipczenko
Text design by Eve Malakoff-Klein

Printed in the United States of America

ISBN # 0–87868–502–2

The work of the CWLA North American Commission
on Chemical Dependency and Child Welfare
and this report were made possible by
the generous support of the J.C. Penney Company.

Contents

Appendices

Acknowledgments

Children at the Front: A Different View of the War on Alcohol and Drugs is the tangible result of 18 months of deliberation by the CWLA North American Commission on Chemical Dependency and Child Welfare. This final report, a collaborative effort, would not have been possible without the talent and commitment of every member of the Commission.

CWLA is especially grateful to Richard L. Jones, Commission Chair, for his even-handed leadership throughout the process. We also could not have succeeded without the knowledge and skills of our subcommittee chairs who kept their groups on task—Sheila Anderson, Larry Mendoza, Elaine Johnson, Ivory Johnson, Lee Dogoloff, Joe Altheimer, and Sheryl Brisset-Chapman. Special thanks also go to those members of the Commission who began this journey in 1989 as members of the original CWLA Chemical Dependency Steering Committee. We want to acknowledge Senator Christopher Dodd (D-CT), and Representatives Major Owens (D-NY) and Joseph Kennedy (D-MA). The Commission benefited immensely from their support and the active involvement of their staff members.

Charlotte McCullough, CWLA Chemical Dependency Program Director, deserves special recognition for her vision in planning the initiative, coordinating the Commission's activities, and creating the framework for this report. We also appreciate the considerable talent and enthusiasm of CWLA staff members—Madelyn DeWoody, Liz Loden, Maureen Leighton, Patrick Curtis, Meredith Moss, Heather Boone, and Mary Liepold—who have provided support to the Commission subcommittees and guidance to the overall initiative.

CWLA is especially grateful to the J.C. Penney Company, whose generous support helped make this publication possible.

Preface

In September 1989, the Child Welfare League of America (CWLA) announced the formation of a Chemical Dependency and Child Welfare Steering Committee comprising 13 experts in child welfare or alcohol and drug abuse chosen from CWLA member agencies. The steering committee was created to set the course and guide the development of this chemical dependency initiative. CWLA member agencies—more than 650 public and voluntary agencies throughout North America—had begun to encounter large numbers of infants exposed in utero to various illicit drugs or alcohol, infants and young children abused or neglected by parents with alcohol or drug problems, and adolescents with dual diagnoses including chronic use of alcohol and other drugs. Those who provide services to strengthen and support families were being challenged as never before by chemically dependent parents. The impact of alcohol and other drugs was leading many professionals inside and outside of the child welfare system to question the effectiveness of existing policies and procedures. Workers needed more training and knowledge in order to make the life-or-death decisions required on a daily basis.

Additionally, at a time when child abuse and neglect reports reached all-time highs and children were at risk as never before because of parents' alcohol or other drug problems, the child welfare system had to confront the reality of inadequate resources—human and financial—with which to address the crisis.

The steering committee discussed, debated, and reached consensus on some of the issues, controversies, and challenges faced by the field. In the spring of 1990, the steering committee held a two-day symposium to share the knowledge and skills they had acquired with a wider audience of child welfare and chemical dependency professionals; to broaden the arena for further debate on legal, ethical, and policy challenges confronting the two fields; and to hear recommendations for the next stage of the CWLA initiative.

The Steering Committee drafted and introduced resolutions related to chemical dependency at the CWLA Biennial Assembly in October 1990. All resolutions were passed, indicating wide support from CWLA's member agencies for the direction of the initiative. Following the Assembly, on the basis of recommendations from the steering committee, CWLA announced the formation of an expanded, high-level, multidisciplinary North American Commission on Chemical Dependency and Child Welfare. (See Appendix B: The North American Commission on Chemical Dependency and Child Welfare.)

In October 1990, the Commission was convened to:

- Further assess the impact of alcohol and other drugs (AOD) on current child welfare policy and service delivery.

- Determine the areas of service delivery requiring additional study.

- Identify core elements of child welfare programs that successfully address chemical dependency issues.

- Determine training needs related to alcohol and other drugs in order to improve practice in all child welfare service areas.

- Debate and resolve AOD and child welfare policies and practices that compromise the ability to deliver quality services.

- Evaluate existing research related to chemical dependency and child welfare. Propose or conduct research needed to determine the true impact of chemical dependency on the child welfare system and the infants, children, youths, and families it serves.

- Make recommendations to improve legislative provisions and agency policies, practices, and programs related to infants, children, youths, and families affected by alcohol and other drugs.

The Commission comprises 70 individuals who came together to discuss the nature of addiction and the best interests of children. Both of these topics strike at the core of professional and personal beliefs and evoke strong reactions. On some issues, there was broad agreement and support from the beginning. In other areas, there were strong differences to be reconciled. During the past 18 months the Commission has met on five occasions, and members have corresponded by phone, fax, and mail between meetings.

Throughout the process, the Commission recognized the complexity of the issues being addressed and rejected the lure of simple solutions generated in a piecemeal fashion. The analysis and debate on all issues, conducted within the framework of existing child welfare law, was child centered and family focused. The process required an examination of the needs of the child at all stages of development and within the context of the family and the community. The Commission's focus on the individual needs of a child and family affected by chemical dependency led directly to the broader issues of how services are currently delivered to children and families and how policies and practices targeted toward the "drug war" relate to those services and to the welfare of children.

The Commission spent much of its time working in four subcommittees: Policy, Practice/ Training Supports, Program Development, and Research. In all groups, many principles underlying good child welfare practice were reaffirmed. Each of the subcommittees made specific suggestions for inclusion in this final report.

Throughout the past year, the members of the Commission have come closer together personally and professionally. An ambitious agenda was embraced; strength grew from different points of view and a common commitment to children and families; and ultimately, even the most difficult issues were addressed. These final recommendations reflect the combined thinking of all Commission members, and taken together, they are a dynamic call to action.

The Commission worked hard to reach consensus on a view of the challenges to the child welfare system posed by family involvement with alcohol and other drugs, and on the steps needed to meet those challenges. This is our common assessment of the problem and our collective vision of a national response. We note, however, that while most members of the Commission support all of the recommendations, some individuals disagree with specific elements of some recommendations in this call to action.

Children at the Front: A Different View of the War on Alcohol and Drugs flows from the guiding principles agreed upon early in the Commission's deliberations. Those principles are based on beliefs about children's needs, the addiction process, the impact of chemical dependency on the family, and the appropriate role of government in meeting children's needs and guarding children's rights.

Following a general introduction (Chapter One), this report links chemical dependency and child welfare in five ways. Chapter Two is an overview of the child welfare system and how it is supposed to protect children and strengthen and support families; it is also an exploration of what chemical dependency means for individuals, families, and service providers.

Chapter Three looks at the challenging service needs of today's chemically involved clients, beginning with an overview of families and chemical dependency. Then it addresses three specific population groups: pregnant and parenting women, drug-exposed infants and toddlers, and adolescents at risk of chemical dependency.

Chapter Four examines the current responses of the child welfare system to these populations and details the eight broad responsibilities of child welfare.

Chapter Five presents an overview of the challenges to related human service systems: alcohol and other drug prevention and treatment providers, child and family courts, the health care system, child day care, and early education.

Chapter Six suggests strategies for improving services to children and chemically involved families at the local community level.

The final chapter, A Call to Action, challenges the President, the Congress, the Department of Health and Human Services (DHHS), governors, and state legislatures to act in behalf of children by taking 12 steps toward child-centered public policies on AOD abuse. The Commission also calls for changes in the policy and practice of the child welfare and related human service systems.

Mission Statement

The North American Commission on Chemical Dependency and Child Welfare is committed to providing the Child Welfare League of America, its member agencies, and other policymakers with culturally competent recommendations and action plans for policy, program development, training, and research regarding the needs of children and families affected by chemical dependency and the child welfare system's response to these needs.

The Commission believes that children are our most valuable resource and that families must be helped to nurture and protect their children. Therefore, the Commission is committed to:

- *Placing the alcohol and drug problems confronting children and families in context.* For the families known to the child welfare system, the problems of chemical dependency, poverty, family and community vulnerability, homelessness, institutional racism, a lack of basic supports, and unequal access to needed services are interrelated. Policy and program development, research, and training decisions must reflect awareness of the larger societal problems that may affect these children and families.

- *Developing responsive policies.* Legislative and agency policies must be consistent with the reality of the lifelong nature of addiction and recovery and the long-term need for support and resources. Policies must support all aspects of a child's development and be responsive to the range of needs that children and their families have at various stages of the addiction process.

- *Increasing the knowledge base and disseminating information.* Extensive, valid, and relevant data are needed to identify effective child welfare responses for different populations. Once developed, this information must be disseminated through multidisciplinary educational, resource, and training materials to professionals throughout the human service system.

- *Developing sound program models and practices.* Child welfare program models and practices must be designed to respond to the long-term needs that alcohol and other drug dependency create for developing children and families. Likewise, the chemical dependency prevention/treatment field must adapt its policies and practices and become committed to promoting healthy family functioning and child well-being. All child welfare and alcohol and other drug services must be delivered in a culturally competent manner.

Guiding Principles

The Commission's task was not unlike that faced by decision makers, providers, and policymakers across the country. When Commission members began to address these complex issues, they had to develop a common language and framework for discussion. The Commission then examined the needs and rights of all children and families who come to the attention of the child welfare system and the responsibilities of various systems to respond. Finally, the Commission looked at the unique needs of chemically involved children and families and the implications for service delivery. This process resulted in the following guiding principles:

1. Child welfare policies, practices, and programs must reflect an understanding of all the factors that positively or negatively affect child development and family systems. Abuse of alcohol and other drugs affects child development and family systems.

Therefore, the child welfare system must understand and address alcohol and other drug abuse and dependency in children and families. Child welfare policies, practices, and programs must:

- respond to the unique needs of children who are affected either by prenatal alcohol or drug exposure or by a host of other detrimental experiences related to their parents' chemical involvement or dependency; and

- respond to the needs of all children entering the system who are themselves chemically involved or at risk of alcohol or drug problems, and prevent children already in the system from becoming chemically involved.

2. Child welfare policies, practices, and programs related to serving all children and families must be guided by research and empirical data. Research suggests that chemical involvement affects children and families differently. Therefore, child welfare professionals must recognize that children and families who are chemically involved are not all alike. The process of assessment, planning, and service delivery must be tailored to match individual needs with appropriate resources.

3. Child welfare laws mandate that services be provided to prevent unnecessary separation of children from their parents; and, when placement is required, to reunite families. When reunification is not possible, children must be given other options for permanency through adoption, another placement intended to be permanent, or adequate preparation for independent living, especially in the case of older adolescents.

Parental chemical dependency does not alter the requirements of state and federal laws. Recommendations for improved services to chemically involved children and families must be addressed within the existing legal framework.

4. Families are important to the development of children, and all children need a sense of belonging. The sense of belonging is usually best promoted in the biological family and within a community that supports a positive cultural and ethnic iden-

tity. This principle is no less true in the case of children of chemically dependent families.

Therefore, the complex needs of the chemically dependent family must be considered in planning for the child. Family involvement is essential and must be supported, beginning with the delivery of preventive services, through treatment and intervention, permanency planning, and final implementation of the permanency plan.

5. All parents coming to the attention of the child welfare system must receive services and supports to prevent unnecessary separation from their children. They must also receive services that support ongoing safe, healthy relationships with their children and facilitate family reunification, when necessary.

Therefore, efforts to support children within their chemically dependent families must attempt to address chemical dependency in the family while meeting the developmental and safety needs of the children. The involvement of chemically dependent parents at all decision-making levels is to be encouraged and supported. Specific services and activities to strengthen and support families will vary with the individual circumstances of the child and family.

6. Many families have multiple problems that require coordinated services and effective case management.

Therefore, child welfare services for chemically involved families should be comprehensive, community based, culturally/ethnically competent, and coordinated through an active case manager who provides linkage with a range of alcohol and drug prevention, treatment, and aftercare services. For many chemically involved families, child welfare must also coordinate efforts with law enforcement, mental health, education, early intervention, and developmental services.

7. Effective delivery of services to all children and families is dependent on a well-trained and well-compensated work force and adequate funding to support an array of services and cross-system approaches.

Therefore, quality services for children and families who are chemically involved must be delivered by staff members, caregivers, and/or volunteers who are representative of the clients served, trained in alcohol and other drug issues as they affect families, able to deliver culturally competent services, and professionally supported to manage the cases they are assigned.

8. Child welfare services must be based on a respect for and sensitivity to the racial, cultural, and ethnic diversity represented in our society. Furthermore, child welfare agencies must identify and help to remedy economic conditions that place the well-being of children and families at risk.

Therefore, child welfare agencies must examine and address racial, cultural, and economic barriers in policies and/or practices that have a negative impact on people of color or poor families. Child welfare professionals must be aware of racial, cultural, and ethnic strengths and traditions that may be drawn upon as resources to promote recovery and prevent relapse. Child welfare providers must advocate for federal, state, and local alcohol and drug policies and practices that are sensitive to the strengths and needs of culturally diverse, economically disadvantaged, or uninsured families.

1

Introduction

The U.S. does not have a coherent policy for children and families. As a nation, we must recognize that our economic growth is tied to whether and when the problems facing children and families are resolved. Our current pattern of neglect is very costly.

—*John D. Rockefeller , IV*
chair, National Commission on Children

The integrity of family life and the well-being of children are being profoundly affected by societal trends. Increasing numbers of Americans are living on the outskirts of hope and opportunity. Although some small segments of our population have enjoyed an improved quality of life, many Americans experience, to some degree, the destructive effects of prejudice, escalating violence, economic erosion, inadequate housing or homelessness, and lack of access to health care. There are increasing numbers of single parents; teen mothers; runaway, "throwaway," or homeless youths; latchkey children; infants and young children abandoned by their parents; and escalating numbers of infants, children, and adolescents needing out-of-home care. The abuse of alcohol and other drugs intensifies these societal ills.

Surveys indicate that our prevention efforts may be effective in reducing alcohol and other drug consumption in mainstream America; however, these trends are not apparent for many of our most vulnerable children, youths, and families. In fact, in many communities, the ravages of illegal drugs have increased. In addition, while drugs and alcohol have been used and abused for decades, in recent years unprecedented numbers of women, including women of childbearing age, have begun to use legal and illegal drugs, resulting in dramatic increases in the numbers of infants born with the effects of in-utero drug exposure.

Dr. Elaine Johnson, director of the Office for Substance Abuse Prevention, has stated in many of her speeches that families are the front line of defense in the "war on drugs." But in too many cases, drugs have broken through the line, and children now stand unprotected at the front. Many of them must live like children of war. They wipe their own tears, eat what they can find, and spend hours or days living at home alone, hiding as best they can from the violence both within their own walls and on the streets of the war zone.

To understand the devastating impact of the drug epidemic on U.S. children, consider the following statistics:

- Over 4.5 million women of childbearing age are current users of illegal drugs.[1]

- An alcohol- or drug-exposed baby is born every 90 seconds.[2]

- Perinatal transmission is the leading cause of HIV infection among children, accounting for 84% of reported pediatric AIDS cases. HIV infection in women is strongly correlated with intravenous drug use by the woman or her sexual partner. In the past year 5,000-6,000 women with HIV infection gave birth. If current trends continue, AIDS will rank among the five leading causes of death among women, children, and adolescents.[3]

According to the most recent national survey, daily, chronic alcohol and drug use and the problems associated with it have increased. In addition, the number of first-time users remains alarmingly high.

- More teen males now die of gunshot wounds than of all natural causes combined. Deaths and violence among adolescents are related to gang activity, spurred by an increasingly aggressive drug trade.[4]

- Emergency room admissions for drug-related problems rose 31% in the most recent six-month period— the largest jump in four years.[5]

- There are more hard-core cocaine users now than there were in 1988. In 1991, weekly cocaine use increased by 29%.[6]

- More than one million people used crack for the first time last year, and 1.2 million people tried heroin for the first time.[7]

- Each year, two to 3 million individuals need, but cannot get, treatment for alcohol or drug problems.[8]

Alcohol and drug abuse are directly related to child and family well-being. Current trends related to family violence, child maltreatment, and the entrance of children into the foster care system dramatically illustrate the relationship.

- Nationwide child abuse reports increased 31% between 1988 and 1990. Parental alcohol and drug abuse is directly related to child maltreatment and family violence.[9]

- In 1983 there were approximately 275,000 children in

out-of-home care. Parental alcohol and drug abuse have contributed to a dramatic increase in the numbers of children requiring out-of-home care.[10] Experts project that in 1995, 550,000 abused, neglected, or abandoned children will be separated from their families and placed in out-of-home care.[11]

- Children under five years old are the fastest growing population in foster care.[12] Infants and young children are also the ones most at risk of maltreatment by a chemically involved parent.[13]

Clearly, the nation's current alcohol and drug policies are not an adequate response to the needs of our most vulnerable children, adolescents, and families. It is time to redefine our priorities and place the needs of children at the forefront of our national alcohol and drug agenda.

These children and their families present American society with complex medical, sociological, and legal dilemmas. We are at a crossroads. A decade after the passage of child welfare reform legislation and five years into the current drug war, the fabric of the human service system is being tested as never before. While the Commission focused on the children in the child welfare system, the well-being of millions of other children and families is also at stake. Policies that fail to address their urgent needs must not be tolerated. It is time to redefine the priorities of the "drug war," build upon existing prevention and treatment efforts, and place the needs of children and their families at the forefront of the national alcohol and drug agenda.

Endnotes

1. U.S. Department of Health and Human Services (DHHS), *National Household Survey on Drug Abuse: Population Estimates 1991*, Washington, DC: DHHS, 1991.

2. Schipper, William, Testimony before the U.S. House of Representatives Select Committee on Narcotics Abuse and Control, July 30, 1991. This figure is based on approximately 350,000 AOD-exposed births, and is lower than many estimates.

3. Pediatric AIDS Coalition, Unpublished 1992 Legislative Agenda, Washington, DC: Pediatric AIDS Coalition, 1992. Based on estimates from the Centers for Disease Control.

4. U.S. Department of Health and Human Services (DHHS), National Center for Health Statistics, "Firearm Mortality among Children, Youth, and Young Adult Populations, Trends and Current Status," *Monthly Vital Statistics Report* 39, 11 (March 14, 1991): 1-5. See also U.S. Department of Justice, Office of Juvenile Gangs, Crime and Drug Trafficking, "Juvenile Justice Bulletin," September 1988, 1-2.

5. Drug Abuse Warning Network (DAWN), National Emergency Room Survey for the first two quarters of 1991.

6. *DHHS National Household Survey* 1991.

7. *DHHS National Household Survey* 1991.

8. National Institute of Medicine, *Treating Drug Problems*, edited by Dean R. Gerstein and Henrick Harwood, Washington, DC: National Academy Press, 1990, 231.

9. National Committee for the Prevention of Child Abuse (NCPCA), Results of the Annual 50-State Survey, 1990, Chicago, IL: NCPCA, 1991.

10. National Commission on Child Welfare and Family Preservation, "A Commitment to Change," Washington, DC: American Public Welfare Association, 1991, 4.

11. U.S. House of Representatives Select Committee on Children, Youth and Families, "No Place to Call Home: Discarded Children in America," Washington, DC: U.S. Government Printing Office, 1989, 19.

12. Wulczyn, Friedhelm, and Goerge, Robert. "A Multi-State Comparison of Placement Histories," Data Presented at the Child Welfare Symposium on Multi-State Foster Care, New York, May 1991.

13. Herkowitz, J.; Seck, M.; and Fogg, C., *Substance Abuse and Family Violence: Identification of Drug and Alcohol Usage During Child Abuse Investigations*, Boston, MA: Department of Social Studies, 1989.

2

An Overview of Child Welfare and Chemical Dependency

Understanding the Multiple Roles of the Child Welfare System

A system may be defined as "units so combined as to form a whole and work, function, or move interdependently and harmoniously."[1] The child welfare system, however, is loosely composed of hundreds of state and county child welfare and family service agencies and thousands of independent, private agencies, and harmony is not always in evidence among them.

Private agencies often provide services to children referred by the public sector through various funding mechanisms. In other instances, children and families access the services of the private agencies without ever coming in contact with public agencies. In some states, public agencies provide the range of child welfare services with little involvement of the private sector. There is no single or standard pattern by which services are organized or delivered at the state or local level, making it impossible to discuss the nation's child welfare system as if it were a coordinated whole.

Child welfare services are often narrowly conceived as child protective services (CPS), foster care, and adoption. In reality, the child welfare system includes services that extend beyond these narrow categories.

Both public and private agencies offer voluntary services to strengthen and support families and prevent maltreatment. Child welfare agencies provide child day care services to millions of children every day. Child welfare professionals find or provide a range of health, mental health, developmental, and case management services for children in the child welfare system, whether or not these children are placed outside their homes. Child welfare agencies provide adolescent pregnancy and parenting services, youth employment and job training, and independent-living services to hundreds of thousands of young adults each year.

Misconceptions also exist about the goals and methods of the legally mandated component of the child welfare system— child protective services, or CPS. CPS is mandated to protect children from abuse or neglect that jeopardizes their physical or emotional well-being. When a report is made to CPS indicating that a child is at risk of maltreatment, the service is required to respond and investigate the allegation. Far too frequently, CPS is thought of only in terms of investigations, rather than as a means to a greater end. The public perception is that an investigation by child protective services results in separation of a child from the family and placement of the child in the foster care system. In fact, the overwhelming majority of children who have contact with CPS do not enter foster care.[2] In some cases, the CPS investigation determines that the child is in a safe and protected environment and the family is not in need of services, and the case is closed. In most situations, the investigation reveals that a risk of maltreatment exists and a determination is made to provide services to the child and/or family to reduce the risk to the child. These cases are often called involuntary service cases; they may or may not be referred to the juvenile court for action. With or without court orders, CPS workers will work with families to define a service plan. For example, parents may be required to participate in alcohol or drug treatment or attend parent training/skill building classes. Families may also receive a range of in-home services designed to assure the safety of the child, reduce risk factors, and improve family stability. Outreach, active case-management, and home visiting are often thought to be effective at this stage.

There is great variability from one jurisdiction to another in the services that are provided to children and families when a CPS case is opened. Across the country, resources for all kinds of services are insufficient and inadequate attention has been given to evaluating what services are essential to protect children and support their families.[3]

When children cannot be protected in their own homes, or when children or adolescents need care or treatment services best provided in an out-of-home care setting, the child welfare system provides an array of temporary, nurturing, out-of-home care options that includes kinship care, family foster care, residential treatment, and group homes. Before, during, and after out-of-home care placement, the child welfare system attempts to help children and families address problems that impair individual and family functioning.

In conclusion, the child welfare system encounters children of all ages. These children come from a diversity of racial, ethnic, and cultural backgrounds and often have multiple physical, emotional, social, medical, and developmental difficulties. They and their families reflect a wide range of both needs and strengths. In response to the incredible variety and range of presenting problems, family compositions, and racial and cultural experiences, child welfare agencies must develop strategies that will effectively protect and meet the needs of all children referred to the system. And the decisions made must take place within the parameters of various legal mandates.

The Federal Legal Mandate: P.L. 96-272

The Adoption Assistance and Child Welfare Act of 1980 (P.L. 96-272) created the legal framework for a comprehensive, systematic response to children at risk and their families. This federal law mandated what many professionals had recognized for decades as "good practice," namely, that children should not be separated from their families except as a last resort. The law is based on the assumptions that children grow best in their own families, that parents have a right to protect their children, that most children can be protected in their own homes, and that most families, given enough support, can be preserved.

The implementation of P.L. 96-272 has demanded a level of accountability previously unknown to the system. In order to be eligible for federal reimbursement, state child welfare agencies must make "reasonable efforts" to prevent the separation of children from parents as well as "reasonable efforts" to reunite the family if out-of-home care is necessary. And, in cases where reunification is not possible or in the best interest of the child, services must be provided to assure "permanency" for the child, i.e., adoption or other placement intended to be permanent or, in the case of many adolescents, transition to independence. Family or juvenile courts are required by this federal law to determine whether the child welfare agency has made such efforts. Most states have laws that require judicial determination of reasonable efforts, but few states have attempted to define what these reasonable efforts are. As a result, there is wide variability among states and agencies in the interpretation of the requirements. The only consistency among the states is in their uniform failure to allocate sufficient resources to meet the requirements of the law.

Changes in Response to P.L. 96-272

The law was intended to reduce the number of children referred unnecessarily to foster care or allowed to be moved from one placement to another without finding a permanent home. Despite inadequate funding, agency policies and practices advanced to benefit many children and families. Workers acquired new skills and learned to make more accurate assessments. Families responded to a host of new family support services. Through intensive efforts and an attitude of respect and support, public and private child welfare professionals succeeded in maintaining and protecting at-risk children in their own homes. Courts and judges, for the most part, embraced the family focus, and policymakers applauded the results of family preservation techniques. The framework of the law, combined with improved programs and services, appeared to be succeeding. In the last few years, however, the needs of children and families have changed, and the systems created to serve them have not been able to achieve the degree of success anticipated when the law was passed. Perhaps the single most significant change is the increase in parental alcohol and other drug (AOD) abuse, particularly maternal AOD abuse, which has radically added to the demands placed on the child welfare system and the related health and human service systems.

It is now apparent that laws alone are not sufficient to protect children and serve the complex needs of their chemically involved parents. A law may prohibit child abuse and neglect, but it cannot prevent or cure it. A law may mandate the rehabilitation of parents, but it cannot rehabilitate them. A law may establish the legal framework for the protection of children, and it can enunciate the philosophy that will motivate and guide a system as it deals with the problems of children and their families. Ultimately, though, the prevention and treatment of the problems, including chemical dependency, which affect children and families, depend less on laws than on the existence of sufficient and suitable services and supports for children and parents. P.L. 96-272 is an essential first step in assuring that children and families receive the services to which they are entitled, but it must be backed up by adequate resources.

Regardless of how state and local child welfare services are delivered, or how adequately they are funded, public and private agencies have eight broad, often overlapping areas of responsibility that fulfill the mission of the child welfare system. These responsibilities are:

1. To protect and promote the well-being of all children.

2. To support families and seek to prevent problems that may result in the neglect, abuse, exploitation, or delinquency of children.

3. To promote family stability by appropriately identifying and assessing family strengths and needs and providing the supports necessary to build on strengths, resolve problems, and safely maintain children in the home.

4. To protect children by placing them in appropriate out-of-home care (which may be kinship care, family foster care, or group/residential care) when continuation in the home would jeopardize the well-being of the child, the family, or the community.

5. To assure that adequate and appropriate services are provided to children in all out-of-home care settings.

6. To reunite families from which children have been separated by providing services to address the problems that led to placement.

7. To place children with adoptive families or in other family care arrangements intended to be permanent, when return to the biological family is not possible or appropriate.

8. To take responsibility for helping to identify and ameliorate the social conditions that negatively impinge on children, such as inadequate housing, poverty, inadequate and inaccessible health care, and chemical dependency.

Conceptual Models for Understanding Chemical Dependency

Societal attitudes and cultural values often dictate how different chemicals are viewed and defined. Since alcohol is legal, widespread, and a part of our social fabric, it is often excluded from discussions about harmful drugs. Yet there is little doubt that alcoholism is a leading drug problem in America today, second only to cigarette smoking as a cause of illness and death. Over 100,000 people die each year from health problems or accidents related to alcohol use.[4] Alcohol abuse is the leading cause of death for persons under 21 years old.[5] Alcohol is frequently implicated in homicides, suicides, and family violence. In addition, most users of illegal drugs also use and abuse alcohol. For all of these reasons, the Commission includes alcohol in the category of chemicals that can cause harm to children and families.

Several interrelated factors must be examined in any serious effort to understand the impact of chemical dependency on individuals, families, or society. Medical, behavioral, and social models are often invoked to understand the etiology of chemical dependency. Each model focuses on selected factors.

The medical model stresses the importance of genetic factors predisposing the individual to dependency. It looks at the addictive properties of the chemical itself and the changes it produces in the central nervous system of the user, and examines the use of chemicals to self-medicate other conditions. The behavioral model examines positive or negative reinforcing factors in the user's environment or in the properties of the chemical that contribute to psychological or physical dependency and cause patterns of use, abuse, addiction recovery, and relapse. The social model emphasizes the importance of external influences such as drug availability, peer pressure, social stress, and other psychosocial factors.

In reality, alcohol and drug dependence and relapse appear to result from a complex combination of all of these interrelated factors. Genetic factors, environmental conditions, the addictive properties of the chemical, reinforcing factors, and psychosocial issues are all critical variables to consider. Effective approaches to chemical dependency operate in the broad context of an individual living in a family that, in turn, functions within a community.

Given the various possible approaches to explaining chemical dependency, there is little wonder that terms and definitions for the condition abound. There are no operationally defined terms, and none that have been approved by the National Institute on Drug Abuse (NIDA). As a result, there is no standard or accepted answer to when use of alcohol or other drugs becomes abuse, or when abuse becomes dependency.

Chemical dependency is often defined by the problems it generates, the danger the problems create, and their persistence. The Commission considered all the factors contributing to chemical dependency and agreed to use the following working definition: Dependence on alcohol and other drugs is a primary, progressive, and chronic condition that can be arrested, but not cured. If left untreated, chemical dependency may be fatal.

> *Primary* means that the chemical dependency* is recognized and addressed as a central issue affecting all aspects of an individual's functioning.
>
> *Progressive* means that the quality of the individual's life will continue to deteriorate if the chemical dependency is not addressed.
>
> *Chronic* means that the dependency is characterized by periods of recovery and often involves relapses over a period of time.

---

* Throughout this document, *chemical* is used to include alcohol and other drugs, and also referenced as AOD; *chemical dependency* is used interchangeably with *addiction*; and use, abuse of, or exposure to any chemical, which may not imply dependency, is described as *chemical involvement*.

Chemical dependency in an individual affects the entire family. Chemical dependency in the parent impairs parenting behaviors. Child welfare interventions, therefore, must address the needs of the child within the context of chemical dependency in the family.

The child welfare system must be concerned about the widespread abuse of alcohol and drugs because chemical dependency affects the entire family and can place children at risk of harm. The chemically dependent person's behavior, self-concept, and relationships become predominantly organized around the use of the chemical. At the same time, family members organize their lives, decision making, perceptions, beliefs, and values around the chemically dependent person and his/her addiction. Alcohol and other drugs thus become the central organizing factor for both the individual and the family.[6]

Chemical dependency in a family should be approached by the child welfare system in the same manner as any other condition or disability that poses a risk to child development, safety, and/or well-being. It should be recognized that parents may engage in different patterns of chemical use or abuse, for varying periods of time, with different consequences for their lives and the lives of their children. Individuals of all ages and backgrounds use and abuse hundreds of mood-altering legal and illegal substances. Aggression or maladaptive behavior may follow the use of alcohol, cocaine, and many other chemicals or combinations of chemicals, whether it be during intoxication, withdrawal, or drug-induced psychotic state. A careful and thorough assessment is, therefore, essential. Moreover, because dependency is preventable and treatable, and because recovery from dependence can improve the quality of family life, prevention efforts, early identification, and referral to appropriate services must be an integral part of child welfare services.

When chemical dependency affects a family, child welfare interventions designed to strengthen or support the family are likely to fail unless they address the alcohol or drug issues. Furthermore, the issues must be addressed in a way that benefits the child and family. Policies or practices that stigmatize or discriminate against a chemically dependent parent will only do further harm to the child and the family. Chemical dependency in the family may be the child's worst enemy, but the dependent parent usually is not. Therefore, child welfare services must attempt to help chemically dependent parents address AOD problems and begin the recovery process. At the same time, child welfare agencies must assure the child's well-being if the parent is unable to provide protection and nurturance to the child. Interventions must strive to minimize the shame and guilt inherent in most chemically dependent parents, while openly addressing the dependency and building healthier parent/child relationships.

Endnotes

1.   *Webster's Unabridged Dictionary*, New York: Simon and Schuster, 1983.

2.   Jones, Beverly, "In Home Services: Substance Abusing Parents," Paper presented at the American Enterprise Institute Conference, July 1991.

3.   Jones 1991.

4.   Centers for Disease Control, *Morbidity and Mortality Weekly Report* 39, 11 (March 23, 1990): 174.

5.   Centers for Disease Control, *Morbidity and Mortality Weekly Report* 40, 48 (December 6, 1991): 821-822.

6.   Brown, Stephanie, *Treating the Alcoholic*, New York: John Wiley and Sons, 1985, 13.

3

Changing Clients, Challenging Needs

The children and families in the child welfare system today are significantly different from those of a decade ago. Children entering foster care, for instance, have more serious or complex needs, and they are more likely to come from highly troubled and/or chemically dependent families. There are more children with multiple diagnoses, serious health problems, mild and moderate mental retardation, and developmental disabilities. There are more infants born with the effects of alcohol or drugs caused by their mother's use during pregnancy, or as a recent report indicated, by paternal drug use at the time of conception.[1] The child welfare system is being flooded by record numbers of CPS referrals for drug-exposed, HIV-infected, or medically fragile infants and young children under the age of six. Infants and young children living with multiproblem, chemically dependent parents are at the highest risk of maltreatment or abandonment. In all age groups, increasing numbers of children are being placed in the foster care system. Once in care, each of these children presents unique challenges to a child welfare system that is already overwhelmed.

Despite rhetoric to the contrary, our society has never made children a priority. Agencies created to serve children and their families have historically lacked the human and fiscal resources to accomplish their missions. This is particularly true for the child welfare system designed to support and protect our most vulnerable children. In the 1960s and '70s thousands of children drifted or languished in the foster care system. Today, in spite of the legal mandates of P.L. 96-272 and new procedures and practices, children continue to remain in care for extended periods of time. Traditional practices that prevented initial placement or achieved family reunification are not as effective or available to children and families as they once were. While chemical dependency in families is certainly not the root cause for the inability of the system to expeditiously achieve a permanent plan for each child in out-of-home care, the needs of today's clients are without doubt adding to, and becoming visible evidence of, a child welfare system in crisis.

What follows are descriptions of the characteristics and service needs of chemically involved children and families coming to the attention of child welfare.

Families and Chemical Dependency

At our best level of existence, we are part of a family, and at our highest level of achievement, we work to keep the family alive.

—*Maya Angelou*
author & playwright

The child welfare system must recognize that chemical dependency in a family affects the well-being of each member of the family. Chemical dependency can permeate all aspects of family life, and can profoundly affect the physical, emotional, and developmental status of children. Chemical dependency can—and does—harm children in any number of ways: through the prenatal exposure of an infant to alcohol or other drugs;

through the creation of a postnatal environment that fails to meet the pressing developmental needs of infants, toddlers, and preschoolers; through children's passive exposure to illicit drugs used in their homes; through active harm caused by violence, sexual assault, neglect, or abandonment; and through genetic and environmental factors that may place children and adolescents at risk of developing chemical dependency problems of their own.

In a chemically involved family, neither parents nor children are likely to have their needs met, so attachment and trust may suffer. Children of all ages require secure attachments to loving parents or other caregivers who are consistent and responsive to their needs. When parents are chemically involved, their children are likely to suffer long-term problems, including school failure, withdrawal, inattentiveness, and behavior problems. If alcohol and drug issues in the family are unaddressed, children may continue to have problems in their relationships with peers and adults, and manifest psychosocial and/or alcohol or drug problems in the future.

Children of parents who are involved with alcohol or other drugs are also at increased risk of both physical abuse and varying degrees of neglect. A chemically dependent parent may behave in ways that jeopardize a child's healthy development. Money, time, and emotional investment often are diverted from the needs of the child to the demands of the addiction. Attention, guidance, and discipline are inconsistent; daily activities have little pattern. Even the child's basic need for safety may be compromised. Under the influence of drugs or alcohol, a parent's thoughts and perceptions may be impaired or distorted, so that memory, attention, and perception are affected.

There are other conditions associated with alcohol or drug abuse in a family that may have negative consequences for children. Depression, for example, is not uncommon as an antecedent or consequence of cocaine or other drug use. Depression, even without associated drug use, has been shown to adversely affect parenting.[2] Alcohol and other drug abuse in a family also significantly increases the possibility that children will witness violence and/or be victims of violence at home. There is increasing concern that exposure to this violence may have serious long-term implications for a child's development.[3]

Children raised in violent alcohol- or drug-involved families may have a diminished ability to concentrate, or have poorly formed attachments, nihilistic or fatalistic orientations toward the future, and a tendency to choose risky behaviors, including the use of alcohol or other drugs, in later life.[4] Preschoolers may be especially vulnerable to traumatic exposure to violence. It is simply wrong to assume that young children will forget or not be harmed by their early experiences.[5]

Service Needs

All families need occasional support and assistance. Chemically dependent families need intensive, immediate, and ongoing assistance to resolve AOD dependency, improve family functioning, and remedy the problems that chemical dependency creates for their children. Children living in chemically dependent families have special needs that are often not heard by service providers. This situation is particularly true in families where the rule of secrecy may be entrenched. Children are often required to keep the family "secret," and as a result are unable to ask for help. They may believe that talking about problems in the family is the most serious form of family betrayal. As a consequence, providers must become sensitized to the issues faced by children whose parents are chemically involved, and be alert to their subtle calls for help. Moreover, providers must intensify AOD education/prevention efforts to ensure that the destructive, intergenerational cycle of addiction is broken. In addition to issues directly related to chemical dependency, other conditions that impede recovery or healthy family functioning must also be identified and remedied.

Conditions that impair parenting and the well-being of children in chemically involved families are of critical importance to the child welfare field. Services must address the chemically involved parent's ability to perceive, understand, and respond appropriately to the needs of her or his children. Interventions such as counseling, parent support groups, parenting education/training, and peer support programs may be required. Services must always address the needs of children at various stages of the parent's addiction and recovery process. While the parent, for example, is attempting to pursue recovery and resolve personal issues that may have preceded chemical abuse, the child's need for love and consistent care remains. The child may also need mental health counseling, developmental services, age-appropriate alcohol and drug education/prevention services, educational assessments, or other special services designed to address unique issues and experiences.

All children should feel safe and secure within their families and in their homes. When chemical dependency threatens that security, services must be provided to the child and family to restore stability and promote optimal development and healthy family functioning. Finally, service providers must address the larger context in which chemical dependency in families arises. Intervention related to parental chemical dependency and services to promote the health and development of a child will be of little avail if the family is faced with drug-related community violence, homelessness, an inadequate income, poor health, unemployment with few job skills or resources, and/or social isolation or alienation. Intervention into this larger social arena presents special challenges and requires a comprehensive and coordinated strategy in which the child welfare system can play an important role.

Chemically Dependent Pregnant and Parenting Women

Within all cultures and socioeconomic situations, there is a biologically driven motivation parents have to care for and nurture their offspring. Yet there are some parents who have priorities that preempt the care and protection of their children.

—*Judy Howard, M.D.*
pediatrician and researcher

The Scope of the Problem

Obtaining precise estimates of the number of women who have AOD problems or of alcohol- and drug-related pregnancies and births is not yet possible. Different researchers, using different methodologies, have examined different drugs or combinations of drugs and alcohol in isolated studies. Among the findings are the following:

- The Institute of Medicine of the National Academy of Sciences estimates that each year from 350,000 to 625,000 pregnant women use one or more illegal drugs during their pregnancies.[6]

- Most abusers of drugs use or abuse multiple drugs and/or alcohol. In one study, 876 pregnant women at three Seattle-area hospitals voluntarily reported the use of various substances. Of those who used cocaine, 82% also drank alcohol, 89% smoked cigarettes, 68% used marijuana, and 33% used other street drugs.[7]

- There is no single "typical" pattern of AOD use during pregnancy. Different patterns and the use of different combinations of drugs have been found to result in different birth outcomes and varying degrees of negative consequences for women and for their infants.[8]

The Demographics of Chemically Involved Pregnant Women

Age and socioeconomic status are the most frequently cited demographics for this population. Pregnant drug abusers identified today are not typically teens. They are in their mid-twenties, and are likely to have one or more children in addition to the identified drug-exposed newborn.[9] Socioeconomic status is not determinative of chemical use in pregnant women. The National Association for Perinatal Addictions Research and Education (NAPARE) demographic survey in Pinellas County, Florida, for example, found no significant difference in rates of drug-exposed births between private and public hospitals and no significant difference in rates of exposure between black and white patients. This study runs counter to the stereotypes regarding users, and gives a clue as to how widespread the problem is among all women of childbearing years irrespective of socioeconomic status. In this same study, however, socioeconomic status and race were related to drug of choice, with lower-income women and women of color more often using cocaine and higher income and Caucasian women using marijuana. Regardless of the drug used, African American women were ten times more likely than Caucasian women to be reported to child welfare.[10]

Effects of Chronic, Daily Alcohol and Drug Abuse

Chronic, daily use of alcohol and other drugs has a profound impact upon the user as well as upon the family. The repercussions are most apparent when the user is a mother who has a new baby and perhaps other young children in the home.[11] In a recently published long-term study of heavily drug-involved mothers, it was found that chemical abuse impaired parenting in a number of ways. These mothers were less sensitive, responsive, and accessible to their infants than mothers without drug involvement. The amount and quality of physical contact was less, as was the acceptance of the infant.

In spite of ongoing case management and family support services, the behavior of the chemically involved mothers continued to deteriorate in all these areas as the infants grew from three to nine months. One hundred percent of the infants showed evidence of insecure attachments toward their drug-involved mothers, and demonstrated fear, anger, or avoidance toward them.[12] Even though most heavily drug-involved women want to be good mothers, they have difficulty doing so. Infants who are born drug- or alcohol-exposed may also be less available for interaction, making it more difficult for mothers who are heavily alcohol or drug involved to provide appropriate levels of stimulation and consistent care.

The Response: Treatment or Punishment?

If these were white middle class women, wouldn't we be talking about Betty Ford programs rather than jail?

—*Ira Chasnoff, M.D.*
president, National Association for Perinatal
Addictions Research and Education (NAPARE)

As the public has become more aware of the plight of babies born to chemically involved women, attempts to monitor or control chemical use during pregnancy have distracted attention from the provision of resources and services these women desperately need. Criminal prosecution of pregnant women for a variety of acts or omissions during pregnancy is the most extreme example of a nontherapeutic intervention. In May 1989, a California woman pleaded guilty to involuntary manslaughter after her premature twins died. She had been smoking crack for two days prior to their birth. In July 1989, a Florida woman was convicted of delivery of drugs to a minor when her baby was born exposed to cocaine.[13] Since that time, approximately 100 cases of fetal endangerment have been entered in 21 states.[14] The adverse effects of legally positioning infants and their mothers as adversaries cannot be ignored.

Carrying this trend even further, drug use has been a factor in the criminal sentencing of pregnant women for crimes unrelated to their drug use or its effect on the fetus. For example, in Washington, DC, a woman pleaded guilty to a first offense forgery charge, a crime which usually results in probation. The judge, however, sentenced her to jail until her baby was born because she tested positive for cocaine.[15]

Nontherapeutic actions may have some initial appeal. The public may be reassured by efforts to reduce the numbers of drug-exposed babies or at least to minimize the damage. These approaches, however, are coming under increasing scrutiny and criticism. Legal experts are voicing concern not only about constitutional issues, but also about the potential flooding of the court systems. Medical experts point out that the threat of legal action will not reduce drug use during pregnancy, but will reduce the number of women who seek treatment or prenatal care. Most importantly, the people at whom fetal abuse statutes and punitive action are targeted are those already locked out of the current health care or treatment systems, including the poor and women of color.

Any punitive action or criminal prosecution of pregnant or parenting chemically dependent women reflects an ambivalence about whether addiction is willful misconduct, criminal behavior, or a treatable disease. Legally, this issue was resolved by the 1962 Supreme Court decision that unequivocally defined chemical dependency as an illness [Robinson v. California 370 U.S. 660].

The Commission strongly opposes nontherapeutic actions and/or criminal prosecution of women, including pregnant women, solely on the basis of their alcohol or drug dependency.

Service Needs of Pregnant and Parenting Women

Early detection, proper prenatal care, medical management, and appropriate AOD treatment services can significantly reduce the damaging effects of alcohol and drugs on the woman and the fetus. The key to effective service delivery is early recognition and the provision of appropriate individualized services both during pregnancy and after the birth of the child.

For many chronic, heavily alcohol- or drug-involved women, long-term residential drug treatment may offer the best hope for recovery. These programs are the ones most likely to address the multiple problems that accompany dependency in many women, who may require "habilitation," rather than "rehabilitation," if they are ever going to become drug free, stay drug free, and be capable of caring for their children in a consistent, healthy manner.

Some communities have acknowledged the need for habilitation programs for chemically dependent pregnant and parenting women, and are attempting to gain priority access to treatment slots for mothers who are primary caretakers for their children or for pregnant women. However, very few women who could benefit from this approach receive the opportunity.

The Pregnant and Postpartum Women and Infants Program of the Office for Substance Abuse Prevention (OSAP) is demonstrating model strategies for overcoming obstacles to providing quality services for women. Residential and outpatient AOD treatment services that allow women to pursue recovery and assume responsibility for their children may be essential in promoting family stability and reducing the risk of future AOD-involved pregnancies. In fact, women who do not get treatment and begin recovery may be more likely to have further drug-exposed births. In San Francisco during the first three months of 1991, drug-exposed births decreased by 17%. However, 95% of these births were to women who had given birth to drug-exposed infants in the past.[16] Women who do not receive treatment and, as a result, lose custody of their children may become pregnant again to "replace" the child they lost to out-of-home care.[17]

The ideal service mix, currently available to only a few

drug-involved women, might include: perinatal case-managed services, developmental follow-up for the children, extensive family support services, AOD education, intervention or treatment services, transportation, child care, parenting training, outreach, aftercare, HIV counseling/testing, family planning counseling, nutritional services for women and their young children, and mental health services. Some women may also require housing assistance, job training, education, or income supports. All pregnant women must have easy access to health education and counseling regarding the effects of tobacco, alcohol, and drugs during pregnancy and the risks associated with HIV infection. All of these services should be available to pregnant or parenting women who need them in order to reduce the likelihood of child maltreatment, maximize each child's developmental potential, support the mother's recovery process, and help her reach her full potential.

The Emergency Child Abuse and Neglect Prevention Program, operated by the Administration for Children, Youth, and Families since FY91, provides grants to state and local family-serving agencies to expand or implement services for the prevention and treatment of child abuse in chemically involved families. Agencies in communities across the nation are using these funds to establish or expand a variety of innovative services. Projects may hire additional personnel, enhance training for personnel to improve the quality of services, expand services to deal with family crises created by alcohol or other drug abuse, and establish or improve interagency coordination.

Barriers to Overcome

Because the pregnant drug user does not usually seek early prenatal care, identification is the first task. Pregnant women, even when they are seen by a social worker or a physician, are not routinely or adequately questioned about chemical use. In the unlikely event that an alcohol or drug problem is acknowledged, the odds of getting into a drug or alcohol treatment program are not in the woman's favor. The more critical the need, the less likely it is that the services will be available. According to one survey, 54% of pregnant addicted women in New York City were refused service by the city's drug treatment programs; 67% were refused if they were on Medicaid; and 87% were rejected if they were pregnant, on Medicaid, and used crack.[18]

Pregnant or parenting chemically dependent women are deterred from pursuing recovery not only by the severe shortage of treatment slots, but also because few treatment programs are set up to meet the unique needs of women. Most residential programs were designed for males. Gender-specific programs sensitive to the needs of pregnant and parenting women and their children have increased in recent years. However, in most communities, these programs are not available, and women have difficulty finding programs which make provisions for child care or for prenatal/postnatal care. Even when providers are willing to allow pregnant or parenting women to keep their children while in residential treatment, the facilities and programs are not usually adapted to meet the needs of children.

Women seeking treatment must also overcome a lack of coordination among community services. Navigating the multiple systems to meet complex medical and social needs is often impossible for the marginally functioning, chemically involved client. As a result, the pregnant alcohol or drug user usually gets no treatment for chemical dependency and receives inadequate medical care.

All of these barriers make it even more difficult for women to deal with the internal psychological dynamics of denial inherent in chemical involvement. Community resistance and a negative perception of pregnant alcohol or drug abusers only solidify this pattern of denial.

In conclusion, specialized treatment and service programs are needed to meet the unique needs of pregnant and parenting women and their children. These programs will require the cooperation and collaboration of multiple service providers.

The "one-stop shopping" model, where drug treatment and maternal and child health services are located in one setting, may be essential to attract women and keep them in treatment.

A number of innovative programs are currently being funded through the Office for Substance Abuse Prevention (OSAP), the National Institute on Drug Abuse (NIDA), the Office of Treatment Improvement (OTI), and the Administration on Children and Families (ACF). However, the demand for services far exceeds the supply.

Infants and Toddlers Prenatally Exposed to Alcohol and Drugs

The public health problem we are facing today kills seven times more neonates every year than the total number who died at the height of the polio epidemic. Yet, there is no sense of outrage surrounding this preventable tragedy!

—Richard Schweiker
former secretary of DHHS
in a letter to President Bush requesting help in
addressing the epidemic of drug-exposed babies

Drug and Alcohol Exposure: How Many Babies?

Firm estimates of the number of babies born exposed to alcohol and other drugs do not exist. Data is lacking partially because maternal drug use and infant symptoms are frequently misdiagnosed or overlooked. Even when they are detected, there is no national system for data collection. Some data, however, are available:

- A recent estimate of the number of newborns prenatally exposed to illicit drugs and alcohol is 554,000 to 739,000 each year.[19]

- Each year, 40,000 babies are born at increased risk of Fetal Alcohol Syndrome (FAS) or Fetal Alcohol Effects (FAE) due to their mothers' drinking during pregnancy.[20]

Costs Associated with Chemically Exposed Infants and Children

The care needed by many chemically exposed infants and children is extraordinarily costly. The cost of a very low birth-weight infant's stay in a neonatal intensive care unit, for example, can reach $150,000 or more. By contrast, the cost of providing prenatal care for a pregnant woman can be as little as $400.[21]

In addition to expensive, intensive medical care at birth, drug-exposed infants often need ongoing medical and social services that will cost billions of dollars. The annual medical cost of caring for cocaine-exposed babies nationwide has been estimated at $33 million for neonates, and as high as $1.4 billion during the babies' first year of life.[22] As the degree of impairment increases, so do the costs. It has been estimated that each seriously impaired alcohol- or drug-exposed infant could need services, including medical care, special education, and related social services, which will cost as much as $750,000 in the first 18 years of life.[23]

Child welfare costs are also rising as the system attempts to respond to the needs of chemically exposed infants. In Illinois alone, the added medical and related costs of caring for 2,500 cocaine-affected babies in child welfare custody last year was $60,000,000.[24] As more chemically affected babies enter the system, costs will continue to spiral upward.

In-Utero Effects of Drugs and Alcohol

It has long been known that factors such as poor maternal health and nutrition, smoking, poverty, and maternal depression all contribute to poor in-utero development. It is within this context that we explore the effects of maternal use of alcohol or other drugs.

The placenta, once thought to be a protective barrier for the developing fetus, is now known to be readily penetrable by any number of toxic and noxious elements. Alcohol and drugs not only cross the placental boundary, but become trapped in the small world of the womb. Their detrimental effects are intensified and prolonged. Prenatal alcohol abuse can cause a condition known as Fetal Alcohol Syndrome (FAS), characterized by prenatal and postnatal growth retardation, central nervous system impairment, and facial dysmorphology. Longitudinal studies have correlated even moderate consumption with a pattern of lesser mental and physical damage known as Fetal Alcohol Effects (FAE).[25]

There is a fairly extensive body of literature on fetal heroin exposure. Documented short-term effects include an increased risk of prematurity, low birthweight, morbidity, and mortality, as well as potentially severe neonatal withdrawal.

Our knowledge of the perinatal effects of cocaine, PCP, and amphetamines is far less complete, but preliminary data and clinical experience suggest grounds for serious concern. Cocaine, like virtually all drugs, easily crosses the placenta, where it is converted into a substance that is actually more potent than cocaine. This altered substance is trapped in the amniotic fluid; the fetus repeatedly ingests and excretes it. Cocaine directly affects the fetus over a much longer time than the time it affects adults. It produces changes in the mother's central nervous system. It is addictive, toxic (causing direct injury), and possibly teratogenic (causing destructive effects on development). Prenatal cocaine exposure has also been correlated by some researchers with growth retardation, spontaneous abortion, premature delivery, *abruptio placentae*, fetal development lags, and underdevelopment of or damage to the cardiovascular, genital and urinary, digestive, and/or nervous systems.[26]

Much of a child's basic neurological and physical development occurs during the prenatal period. When mental and physical development is disrupted by the mother's use of chemicals, a child's intellectual and developmental outcome is compromised.

Characteristics of Prenatally Chemically Exposed Infants

Babies exposed in utero to alcohol, crack, and other drugs are not all affected similarly. Those suffering the most extreme effects are recognizable at birth, with approximately 18% requiring intensive care.[27] In most cases, however, the effects of in-utero exposure are much more subtle, and the newborn may present at birth with no symptoms. In fact, as many as 70% of these newborns may appear healthy; others may demonstrate mildly disorganized developmental patterns.[28]

The range in severity of impairment is thought to be related to a number of prenatal factors including the type of drugs used, the characteristics of the drugs (i.e., whether they were addictive, toxic, teratogenic, or a combination), the time and frequency of use, the general health and genetic history of the mother, and the prenatal care history. Paternal drug use may also be implicated. Those children most at risk of impairment come from highly dysfunctional, heavily drug-involved families, where chemical abuse is only one of a multitude of problems.

The postnatal environment may exacerbate or reduce existing problems. Postnatal environments where parents are chemically involved may pose a risk to the child in the form of neglect or inattention to nutrition or health needs. In addition, the infant's need for interaction and stimulation may be compromised. In the worst case scenario, the infant is at risk of abuse or maltreatment, passive exposure to illicit drugs, and the chaos associated with drug use and community violence.

Even in the best environments these infants may be difficult to care for and nurture, particularly those who are irritable, hypo- or hypersensitive to stimuli, resistant to cuddling, and prone to high-pitched screaming. Many drug-exposed infants have significant feeding and sleeping problems throughout the first six months of life.[29] Protracted crying, frantic sucking, tremors, and an inability to organize normal sleep-wake cycles are frequently observed. Infants exposed prenatally to heroin or methadone may suffer ongoing vomiting and diarrhea. Children exposed to cocaine and other stimulants may exhibit feeding and sleep difficulties, excessive sucking, and poor weight gain. Parents may have difficulty coping and relating positively to infants who exhibit these behaviors. Researchers employing a range of diagnostic tools to assess drug-exposed infants have concluded that the behavior patterns of some of these neonates are likely to tax the ability of any caregiver to adapt to the infant.[30] Intervention strategies must counterbalance all of the interrelated factors that place the infant's development at risk.

Long-Term Effects of Prenatal Exposure

During the second half of the first year, the majority of alcohol- or drug-exposed infants do begin to organize their sleep-wake cycles, have less difficulty with feeding, and appear to have recovered from the developmental effects of their prenatal exposure. When standardized developmental evaluations are administered and the motor, cognitive, language, and personal-social areas of behavior are assessed, however, these children as a group score within the low normal range, while matched non-drug-exposed groups score within the medium normal range.[31]

As prenatally exposed children grow, concerns begin to emerge about the more subtle behaviors that may influence successful learning experiences and productive adult life. For example, some drug-exposed two-year-olds have been reported to have difficulty concentrating, interacting with others, and coping with structured environments. In somewhat older drug-exposed children, researchers have documented attention deficits, hyperactivity, impulsive behaviors, aggressiveness, and difficulties in making friends and handling social interactions.[32] It is not clear to what extent these observed characteristics are the result of prenatal exposure or are the result of low birth weight, inconsistent or inadequate caregiving, or other factors. The complex interplay between the prenatal and postnatal environments is not yet fully understood. More rigorous study is needed to determine the actual effect of prenatal chemical exposure.

Developmental Needs of All Infants and Toddlers

For all children, development is a cumulative process that begins before birth and continues into young adulthood, but the first three years are critical. These years are a time of extraordinary and unparalleled physical, intellectual, social, and emotional development.

Of particular importance is the infant's need for healthy attachments. In the first few months of life, infants need to begin to develop strong, secure attachments to their primary caregivers, usually their parents. These attachments do not occur automatically or instantaneously. They must be nurtured over time by consistent, loving attention to the infant's needs provided by caring adults. This process is facilitated over time by the dynamic interaction between an alert, responsive baby and a consistent, capable caregiver. Children who are drug exposed might not be alert or responsive, and their caregivers, if chemically involved, might not be consistent or capable. When children are denied opportunities to develop these early significant attachments, they are at much higher risk of significant developmental delays and impairments in their ability to develop healthy relationships in later life.

Environments to Maximize Optimal Development

Good care of children goes beyond food and clothing. All babies and young children need to be held securely, to be interacted with, to be allowed to rest. The parent or caregiver must be able to monitor the child's behavior, read subtle or confusing cues, and respond appropriately in order to minimize distress and increase contentment. It is through this day-to-day interaction that the infant begins to develop a sense of trust in him/herself and an attachment to the primary caregiver(s).[33]

Erik Erikson describes the attachment process as one in

which the primary experience of the child is "taking in." The infant takes in not only nutrients but also a parent's attention, as sights, sounds, touch, texture, smells, and warmth. In the best scenario, the parent functions as a protective barrier, filtering the child's experiences so they are neither too sparse nor too overwhelming. The parent helps the child begin to organize the world in a manageable and predictable way.[34]

Clearly, the order, predictability, and loving, consistent care that most children receive at birth and build upon throughout their lives may not be available to infants born to chemically dependent parents. The postnatal environment may be an assault on all of the child's senses. Children may find themselves in a world characterized by unpredictability and extremes. They may be underattended to or overly stimulated; their needs may be unrecognized; and they may learn not to trust themselves or their caregivers to find order in the world around them.

Service Needs

Chemically exposed infants and toddlers may face substantial risks to their health and well-being from prenatal exposure to chemicals and, more importantly, from postnatal factors related to ongoing parental chemical dependency. Some researchers believe that infants who have been prenatally exposed to drugs may be at greater developmental risk from their postnatal environment than from the prenatal drug exposure.[35] Services, therefore, must be centered around the child's need for a safe, secure, predictable environment where medical needs are met and opportunities are provided to compensate for neurodevelopmental immaturities. To maximize the potential for an appropriate attachment, these children must have stable, loving, consistent, interactive caregiving over time.

A recent study sponsored by the National Institute on Drug Abuse (NIDA) and conducted by the National Association for Perinatal Addictions Research and Education

(NAPARE) provides a clear indication of the way in which services must be provided to this population. This longitudinal study of the developmental progress of 300 children who had been prenatally exposed to illicit drugs had three major findings:

- Almost 100% of the infants tested within the normal cognitive range.

- Although 100% of the children exhibited neurobehavioral deficiencies as infants, by the age of three or four, the majority had achieved levels of social, emotional, and intellectual development that placed them within the normal range.

- About 30-40% of the cocaine-exposed children, however, continued to display problems in language development and/or attention. The additional problems included low thresholds for overstimulation and frustration, poor impulse control, and withdrawal.

The overall positive findings in this study were linked to the presence of several mitigating factors. The mothers in the study received treatment for their addiction. Intervention, treatment, and prenatal care began during the pregnancy; consequently, there were fewer babies with low birthweights. After birth, the mothers voluntarily participated in well baby clinics. Parents and caregivers were given advice and training on how to handle and care for the infants. As the children grew and their needs changed, the parents were taught techniques for providing consistent, structured, and predictable care. When indicated, children were referred to physical therapy, speech therapy, and Head Start programs. Parents were given help with transportation and child care for siblings.[36]

All of these factors contributed to positive outcomes for most of the children in this program; but the positive outcomes in this study are in stark contrast with the reality for most pregnant or parenting drug users and their infants. Most women are not able to get drug treatment. Many AOD-exposed infants are discharged from the hospital into environments that exacerbate their neurobehavioral problems. Most families cannot gain access to any of the supportive services provided to the families in the study.

In conclusion, all children born exposed to alcohol or other drugs while in utero are at risk of experiencing developmental delays and lifelong complications. They must have a chance for comprehensive, integrated interventions that include social, health, child welfare, and educational services. Failure to address these complex interrelated needs through intensified prevention and early intervention services exacerbates the problems, and makes them far more expensive, in human and financial costs, to rectify.

Adolescents at Risk

Although the majority of young people emerge from adolescence healthy, hopeful, and able to meet the challenges of adulthood, many young people experiment with what they take as credentials of adulthood—alcohol or other drugs; violent, dangerous, or illegal activities; and sexual activity—often with dire, if not fatal consequences.

—The National Commission on Children

Adolescence is a turbulent period in the human life cycle, often characterized by mood swings, ambivalence, experimentation, and a search for identity. All adolescents need support to make the passage into adulthood. Without positive relationships with adults, feelings of self-worth, dreams for the future, and opportunities for achieving them, some adolescents may turn to alcohol or other drugs. A large percentage of adolescents who abuse chemicals have a history of physical, sexual, or emotional abuse in the family.[37] Chemical use makes life even more confusing and stressful for these young people.

In addition to preventing and treating chemical use in

adolescents, it is necessary to acknowledge that many adolescents engage in drug trade prior to drug use. The economics of addiction and the implications for prevention, treatment, and aftercare strategies are just beginning to receive serious attention by policymakers and program developers.

The Scope of the Problem

Despite some recent reversals and some cause for optimism regarding adolescent chemical dependency, the U.S. still has a serious problem. In 1991, 6.8% of all adolescents 12 and over had used an illicit drug during the past month.[38] Over 1.2 million adolescents used drugs in 1991.[39] Among high school dropouts, illicit drug use is even more prevalent. Almost 17% of dropouts had used an illicit drug within the past month.[40] Young adults between 18 and 25 have the highest rates of marijuana and cocaine use.[41] In addition, an estimated 4.6 million adolescents—three out of every 10—have alcohol problems.[42] One in four teens engages in other high-risk behaviors that endanger health and well-being. The number of violent youth offenders has also soared as gang activity has increased. Deaths, violence, and gangs are spurred by the aggressive drug trade that permeates many communities. Violence and injury, often related to alcohol and drug use, are responsible for 75% of adolescent deaths.[43] In a study in which teens who used drugs reported on violent events in their lives, responses revealed that teenagers who use drugs had participated in violent acts more frequently than non-drug-using teens.[44] All told, it is estimated that seven million young people have multiple problems, including chemical dependency, that limit their futures.[45]

Risk Factors Associated with Adolescent Use of Alcohol or Drugs

Although we cannot yet predict who will develop a drug or alcohol problem, there are certain factors that place adolescents at increased risk of use and abuse. Factors associated with "use" appear to be different than the factors associated with "abuse." Peer and community social influences are the best predictors of use. Other factors related to use include parent and sibling drug use, inconsistent family relationships, social deprivation, school failure, frequent moves, skill deficits, and antisocial behavior. Abuse of drugs is more closely linked with genetic or family factors and psychological problems that might lead the teen to self-medicate against distress or seek escape through drug highs.

Adolescent women who use or abuse drugs often engage in other behaviors that put them at risk of unwanted pregnancy. An estimated 11% of female adolescents aged 15 to 19 become pregnant each year. Adolescents account for one-third of all unintended pregnancies.[46] All pregnant women must have easy access to health education and counseling regarding the effects of tobacco, alcohol, and drugs during pregnancy. AOD-involved adolescents must be made aware of the high risk of sexually transmitted diseases, including HIV infection and AIDS.

The Office for Substance Abuse Prevention (OSAP) has identified certain groups of adolescents at "high risk" for developing AOD problems:

- children of alcoholics and drug users;

- victims of physical, sexual, or psychological abuse;

- school dropouts;

- pregnant teenagers;

- economically disadvantaged youths;

- youths with mental health problems, including depression;

- physically or mentally challenged youths;

- gay and lesbian youths;

- runaway and homeless youths; and

- children in out-of-home care.

Only a small percentage of all adolescents who have chemical abuse problems are found in alcohol or drug treatment programs. Many substance-involved adolescents are in juvenile justice and runaway programs. Others are in the midst of the homeless or "throwaway" population. Anecdotal reports suggest that over half of the adolescents entering the child welfare system have used or abused alcohol or other drugs. Most chemically involved adolescents live at home, hiding their alcohol or drug problems in a pattern of denial.

A Special "At Risk" Group: Runaway, Throwaway, and Homeless Youths

National estimates indicate that there are as many as 1.3 million runaway, throwaway, or homeless youths in the U.S. today. These numbers are based largely on the numbers of youths who seek shelter, so they may understate the problem of countless invisible street kids.[47] The terms *runaway, throwaway,* and *homeless* are often used interchangeably, but that blending of terms belies the great variability of this population. Runaway, throwaway, and homeless youths do not fit a single mold. Some have families to whom they can return, but an increasing number do not. For many, if not most, efforts spent on reunification are futile. Many adolescents in this group have been "thrown away" not just by their families, but also by the systems created to serve them. Some leave the child welfare system when an arbitrary date on a calendar indicates they are ready for independence. Others are rejected before ever gaining entrance into the system. Too often, the increasing numbers of very young children in critical need of protection have made the child welfare system blind to the urgent, if not life-threatening, needs of adolescents. As many as half of today's street children were yesterday's child welfare children.[48]

Not surprisingly, alcohol and drug abuse rates in this population have consistently remained higher than in the general population. There are more users, more who engage in drug trade, more victims of drug violence, more polydrug use, and a higher chance that these adolescents are using chemicals to self-medicate other serious conditions, including severe depression. Of equal importance is the fact that female runaways are now outnumbering males in some runaway programs. Increasing numbers of girls and young women are engaging in unprotected sex, thus placing themselves at risk of unintended pregnancies and sexually transmitted diseases, including HIV infection. They and their babies are at extremely high risk of medical complications before and at birth.

Adolescents at risk of chemical dependency are served by many different systems, but typically, programs established to help adolescents with one presenting problem, such as poor health, depression, delinquency, emotional problems, or homelessness, do not focus on an accompanying chemical dependency problem or provide any help in dealing with it. This categorical approach to service delivery is typical of the child welfare system, which serves increasing numbers of these children and youths.

For some time, child welfare providers have been describing the "tougher kids" that they see in care. These tend to be adolescents with a history of juvenile justice contacts, multiple offenses, school failure, violence, and highly dysfunctional families. They frequently have other serious mental health, physical health, or behavioral problems. There is a growing awareness of the issue of "co-morbidity"—the coexistence of multiple emotional or mental health problems and chemical use—and the incredible challenge it poses for all service providers.

By creating the "high-risk youth" category, OSAP is alerting providers and community leaders to the critical and often invisible needs of these children and to the need for active prevention and intervention services. OSAP high-risk youth programs now serve as models for comprehensive, collaborative efforts for these children. Chemical dependency is interrelated with the adolescent's other presenting problems, so effective strategies must look at the total child in the context of family and community.

The child welfare system is also beginning to recognize the connection between unintended pregnancy and the use of alcohol and other drugs. Greatly expanded efforts are needed in addressing sexuality and providing family planning assistance to young men and women. All adolescents should receive information about the dangers of unprotected sex and use of alcohol or other drugs and the risk of HIV/AIDS. Standard medical protocols and training of health care providers in identification and effective intervention with adolescents are also essential.

Service Needs

In every city in America, there is a shortage of appropriate, accessible, affordable mental health and alcohol and drug treatment programs. Adolescents in need of alcohol or drug treatment who are ineligible for Medicaid or have no medical insurance have very limited, if any, access to treatment. The problem is particularly acute in areas with a large urban low-income population. There are few communities where a well-developed continuum of services is available at low cost to low-income adolescents and their families. There are no states with comprehensive statewide systems providing the full range of services for adolescents, although states such as North Carolina, Wisconsin, and Washington have begun to explore some innovative treatment strategies.[49] As one strategy for expanding services, states can expand Medicaid services for chemically involved adolescents by adding new optional services to the state's Medicaid plan and by revising definitions of existing services to specifically include services to adolescents. However, any changes of this nature must be accompanied by additional state revenues to pay the state's matching share, which will range from 20% to 50% of the costs of new or expanded services.[50]

In conclusion, despite the most recent high school survey, which revealed an overall decline in drug use, adolescent chemical dependency remains a critical problem that such surveys may fail to capture. Prevention and treatment efforts appear to be addressing the needs of mainstream youths and their families, but these efforts may not be reaching the youths most at risk of chemical dependency. National statistics on teen use are collected in such a way as to eliminate many adolescents who are not living in "households." Runaway, throwaway, and homeless youths, and children in child welfare residential or group homes or juvenile justice facilities are at particularly high risk of developing an alcohol or drug problem. The nature of existing national surveys, however, makes it difficult to track the prevalence and trends of alcohol or drug problems in the high-risk youth segment of our population.

Endnotes

1. Abel, Ernest L. "Paternal Exposure to Alcohol." In *Perinatal Substance Abuse: Research Findings and Clinical Implications*, edited by T.B. Sonderegger. Baltimore, MD: Johns Hopkins (in press).

2. Zuckerman, Barry, "Heavy Drug Users as Parents: Meeting the Challenge," Paper presented at the American Enterprise Institute Conference, July 1991.

3. Zuckerman 1991.

4. Zuckerman 1991.

5. Zuckerman 1991.

6. Institute of Medicine, *Treating Drug Problems*, edited by Dean R. Gerstein and Henrick Harwood, Washington, DC: National Academy Press, 1990, 85.

7.   Streissguth, A. P.; Grant, T.M.; Barr, H.M.; Brown, Z.A.; Martin, J.C.; Mayoch, D.E.; Ramey, S.L.; and Moore, L., "Cocaine and the Use of Alcohol and Other Drugs During Pregnancy," *American Journal of Obstetrics and Gynecology* 164, 5 (May 1991): 1239-1243.

8.   Zuckerman, Barry, "Drug Exposed Infants: Understanding the Medical Risks," *The Future of Children* 1 (Spring 1991): 27.

9.   U.S. Department of Health and Human Services (DHHS), Office of the Inspector General, "Crack Babies," Washington, DC: U.S. Government Printing Office, February 1990, 9.

10.   Chasnoff, I.J.; Landress, H.J.; and Barrett, M.E., "The Prevalence of Illicit Drug or Alcohol Use during Pregnancy and Discrepancies in Mandatory Reporting," *New England Journal of Medicine* 322 (1980): 1202–1206.

11.   Howard, Judy, "Heavy Substance Abusers as Parents: Results of An Early Intervention Approach," Paper presented at the American Enterprise Institute Conference, July 1991.

12.   Howard 1991.

13.   Horowitz, Robert, "Parental Substance Abuse: Legal Issues for Child Protection Intervention," *Protecting Children* 6, 4 (Winter 1989–1990): 21–23. See also English, Abigail, "Prenatal Drug Exposure: Grounds for Mandatory Child Abuse Reports," *Youth Law News* XI (Special Issue, 1990): 3–8.

14.   Personal Communication, Lynn Paltrow, Reproductive Freedom Project, American Civil Liberties Union, New York, February 1992.

15.   Horowitz, Robert, "Pre- and Post-Substance Abuse: Legal Issues and Considerations," Testimony before the U.S. House of Representatives Committee on Ways and Means, April 3, 1990.

16.   DelVecchio, R., "Bay Area Crack Baby Epidemic Declines," *San Francisco Chronicle,* June 3, 1991, A-13.

17.   Barth, Richard P., "Protecting Children of Heavy Drug Users: A Call for Sustained Protection and Prevention Services,"

Paper presented at the American Enterprise Institute Conference, July 1991.

18. Chavkin, Wendy, "Drug Addiction and Pregnancy: Policy Crossroad," *American Journal of Public Health* 80, 4 (1990): 483–487.

19. Gomby, D. and Shiono, P, "Estimating the Number of Substance-Exposed Infants," *The Future of Children* 1, 1 (Spring 1991): 17. This figure includes all children born to women who used alcohol or drugs, and does not imply that all of these children will be impaired by the prenatal exposure.

20. National Association of State Alcohol and Drug Abuse Directors (NASADAD), *Treatment Works: A Review of 15 Years of Research Findings*, Washington, DC: NASADAD, 1990, 7.

21. The National Commission on Children, *Beyond Rhetoric: A New American Agenda for Children and Families*, Washington, DC: U.S. Government Printing Office, 1991: 122.

22. Burnison, Judith, Testimony before the U.S. House of Representatives Select Committee on Narcotics Abuse and Control, July 30, 1991.

23. General Accounting Office, *Drug-Exposed Infants: A Generation at Risk*, Washington, DC: U.S. General Accounting Office (GAO/HRD-90–138), June 1990, 35.

24. Burnison 1991.

25. Streissguth, Ann, "Fetal Alcohol Syndrome and the Teratogenicity of Alcohol: Policy Implications," Paper prepared for the 8th World Congress of the International Commission for the Prevention of Alcoholism and Drug Dependency, September 1991 (in press).

26. Finnegan, L.P., "Outcome of Children Born to Women Dependent on Narcotics," *The Effects of Maternal Alcohol and Drug Abuse on the Newborn*, edited by B. Stimmel, New York: Haworth Press, 1982, 55–102. See also Howard, J.; Kropenske, V.; and Tyler R., "The Long-Term Effects on Neurodevelop-

ment in Infants Exposed Prenatally to PCP," *Phencyclidine: An Update*, National Institute on Drug Abuse Research Monograph Series 64, Rockville, Maryland: NIDA, 1986.

27. Halfon, Neal, Testimony before the U.S. House of Representatives Select Committee on Children, Youth and Families, May 17, 1990.

28. Halfon 1990.

29. Deren, Sherri, "Children of Substance Abusers: A Review of the Literature," *Journal of Substance Abuse Treatment* (1986): 77–94.

30. Howard, Judy, "Perinatal Substance Abuse," in *A Handbook on Drug Abuse Prevention* (in press).

31. Howard 1992. See also Howard, J., and Beckworth, L. "The Development of Young Children of Substance Abusing Parents: Insights from Seven Years of Intervention and Research," *Zero to Three* 9, 5 (June 1989): 8-12.

32. Howard 1992.

33. Benoit, M.B., "The Holding Environment that Children Need," Paper presented at the American Enterprise Institute Conference, July 1991.

34. Benoit 1991.

35. Benoit 1991; see also Zuckerman 1991, and Howard 1991.

36. Burnison 1991.

37. Henry, P.B., Preface to *Special Problems in Counseling the Chemically Dependent Adolescent*, edited by Eileen Sweet, New York: Haworth Press, 1991, xvi.

38. U.S. Department of Health and Human Services (DHHS), National Household Survey on Drug Abuse: Population Estimates, 1991.

39. DHHS National Survey 1991.

40. DHHS National Survey 1991.

41. DHHS National Survey 1991.

42. NASADAD 1990: 7.

43. American Medical Association, (AMA), *America's Adolescents: How Healthy Are They?* Chicago, IL: AMA, 1990, xi.

44. Carpenter, Cheryl; Glassner, Barry; Johnson, Bruce; and Loughlin, Julia, *Kids, Drugs, and Crime*, Lexington, MA: Lexington Books, 1988, 90.

45. National Commission on Children 1991: xxvii.

46. AMA 1990, 43.

47. "Substance Abuse and Homeless, Runaway, and At-Risk Youth," Fact Sheet published by the National Network of Runaway and Youth Services (NNRYS), Washington, DC: NNRYS, 1990.

48. Pires, Sheila A., and Tolmach, J., *On Their Own: Runaway and Homeless Youth and Programs That Serve Them*, Rockville, MD: National Institute on Drug Abuse and National Institute of Mental Health,1991.

49. Ooms, T., and Herendeen, L., "Adolescent Substance Abuse Treatment: Evolving at Federal, State, and City Levels," Background Report and Meeting Highlights, Family Impact Seminar, Washington, DC, November 1989.

50. Ooms 1989.

4

Current Responses of the Child Welfare System

> The challenge is not simply to reduce risk factors that threaten children's futures but to overcome them by identifying and building in protective factors.
>
> *—The National Commission on Children*

Given the realities that now threaten the health and welfare of children and the absence of a comprehensive array of services to assist families, the child welfare system is being asked to intervene and, in effect, to "fix" family problems on multiple fronts. This expectation is heard at a time when federal and state policies have resulted in budget limitations. Programs and staff have been caught between fiscally driven cutbacks and need-based demands for services. The urgency of the cases demands that workers be supported to fulfill their legal and professional responsibilities.

The system has never been given adequate resources to meet the demands placed on it. Recent problems with chemical dependency have merely exacerbated long-standing problems within the system. Many child welfare staff members, foster parents, and child day care providers do not have knowledge of the effects of alcohol and other drugs, or the skills, training, supervision, or support to effectively serve chemically involved families. A series of other obstacles is also jeopardizing the system's ability to protect and serve at-risk infants and children and chemically involved youths.

Many of the current obstacles to quality services are due to shortages: a lack of workers to handle the referrals; a lack of collaborative, community-based efforts; a lack of skilled foster parents; a lack of courts and judges equipped to make sound decisions regarding chemically involved families; a lack of adequate resources, including available, accessible drug treatment for uninsured or indigent people; a lack of coordination of existing services and systems of care; a lack of available options when the decision is made to separate a child from a family; and often, a lack of consensus as to what the parents need and what is in the best interests of the child.

All these shortages exist at a time when the overall trends for child welfare are quite alarming. Many of these trends directly correlate with chemical dependency:

- Nationwide child abuse reports increased 31% between 1985 and 1990.[1]

- For the period between 1989 and 1990, 2.5 million children were reported to CPS agencies as victims of child maltreatment. This is about 39 of every 1,000 U.S. children.[2]

- The surge in CPS referrals has resulted in backlogs of uninvestigated cases, with many workers carrying caseloads in excess of 50 cases.[3] CWLA standards call for no more than 12 to 17 cases.[4]

- Alcohol and other drugs are frequently factors in child maltreatment. Studies show that abuse or neglect of very young children is particularly associated with parental drug use. A Boston study found that AOD use was a factor in 89% of the abuse cases involving infants.[5]

- Since 1985, reports of child fatalities due to maltreatment have increased 38% nationwide.[6]

- By 1995, an estimated 550,000 children will be in foster care. Almost 100,000 children will live in juvenile justice facilities and another 55,000 will receive inpatient or residential treatment for mental health problems.[7]

- Although children in out-of-home care come from all racial and ethnic groups, children of color and poor children are overrepresented in the child welfare population.[8]

In examining how well the child welfare system is currently serving the new populations, it is necessary to look at the array of services and programs needed to fulfill the major responsibilities of the system. This chapter addresses each of these responsibilities and the special challenges created by children and families who are involved with alcohol or other drugs. Each section analyzes a distinct service area of the system.

Preventing Child Maltreatment and Chemical Abuse

To be effective in providing prevention and early intervention services to children and families at risk because of chemical dependency, the child welfare system must work closely with other agencies and systems, including the AOD treatment, legal, medical, mental health, educational, and law enforcement communities. Adequate resources, coordination, and a shared purpose among these different systems and agencies are frequently missing.

In the initial stages of a parent's chemical dependency, children may be neglected while he or she pursues drug-related activities, but they may not be at imminent risk of life-threatening harm. Unfortunately, at this early stage, when prevention and early intervention services have the greatest potential for success, the child welfare system has few resources available to strengthen or support the family. These neglect cases are often themselves neglected until parental drug involvement escalates, pushing fragile families over the edge, creating the potential for serious endangerment.

This organizational neglect is due in part to the reality that CPS assessments take a major portion of many public child and family agency budgets. Resources for prevention, early intervention, and ongoing support services to families not yet in crisis are elusive. The limits on staff resources mean that workers may only attend to the most urgent cases and cannot respond to chronic family problems until they become more acute. The risk to many vulnerable children is consequently heightened and the crisis escalated.

In addition to preventing child maltreatment, child and family service providers should attempt to foster child and family well-being and prevent the escalation of alcohol or drug problems by providing services of many kinds.

Services to Maximize the Developmental Status of Children

Because the diagnostic tools that are presently available cannot detect many of the difficulties that drug-exposed toddlers and preschoolers might experience at various developmental stages, there is great inconsistency in the type and extent of early interventions used by the child welfare system in working with this population, and little evaluative data to assess effectiveness.

Creative, but isolated efforts are underway. These include attempts to team child welfare workers and public health providers in aggressive outreach to newborns and mothers after discharge from the hospital. These projects, however, tend to be underfunded or supported by short term grants, and they are not widely available. Far greater resources must be devoted to these efforts.

Specialized Child Day Care

Child day care can be an oasis within the community for nurturance, stability, and positive stimulation and relationships for the child. It is also essential for parents who seek community alcohol or drug treatment services but cannot participate without access to child day care.

The nation's child day care providers are in daily contact with millions of families who voluntarily seek their service. Day care providers are an underutilized resource for identifying families and children in need of alcohol or drug treatment or referral services. Given adequate training and supports, child day care providers could greatly enhance a community's AOD prevention and treatment efforts. Specialized child development services, made available throughout the country, could improve the developmental outcome for many alcohol- or drug-exposed children, and provide an essential support to families coping with AOD problems or in treatment or recovery programs.

Alcohol and Other Drug Prevention Efforts

Because the child welfare system is mandated to fulfill other functions, it has had few, if any, resources with which to deliver the primary prevention services necessary to effectively prevent parental chemical dependency or initiation of drug use by children and youths in the child welfare system. The challenge is to assess the resources within the child welfare system that can be allocated so that meaningful primary prevention services can be rendered, and/or ensure referral mechanisms and interagency collaboration so that parents and their children have access to such services. Child welfare must explore opportunities to coordinate prevention strategies with other agencies and systems. These might include the public health, housing, income assistance, vocational rehabilitation, mental health, chemical abuse treatment, and educational systems.

Making Accurate Assessments

In order to fulfill its many and varied responsibilities, the child welfare system must make culturally competent, accurate assessments at various points in the decision making and service delivery process. Data collected and analyzed by child welfare is critically important to juvenile and family courts in fulfilling their responsibilities under the law. Other related health or human service providers must also be prepared to assess the impact of alcohol and other drug abuse on the child and family and to share with child welfare the results of their examinations.

Without knowledge of the effects of alcohol and drugs and understanding of the various patterns of use and the addiction process, child welfare professionals and others are unable to make accurate assessments. Without this information, service providers are limited in their ability to determine service needs and provide appropriate interventions.

Child Protective Service Risk Assessments

Risk assessment is central to child protective service decision making. Whenever a report of abuse or neglect is filed, CPS workers must assess the current and potential risk of harm to a child.

In assessing risk when parental alcohol or drug use is a factor, workers must determine the nature of the chemical involvement, the duration and frequency of use, the presence of other underlying problems exacerbated by chemical use, the willingness to participate in drug treatment, the level of motivation and commitment to parenting, the support of the family or community, the availability of appropriate drug treatment services, and a host of other non-drug-related factors that all affect the ability to parent a child. In addition to these factors, the assessment must also explore the level of attachment and closeness between the parent and child and other potential family strengths.

It is important for those conducting the assessment to recognize that the daily activities of chemically dependent individuals may be driven by drug-related pursuits. Alcohol or drug abusers may miss appointments and appear not to cooperate with the investigation and assessment processes. The use of some chemicals, such as crack, may result in bizarre, unpredictable, or even violent behavior. Perhaps most importantly, those conducting the assessment must recognize denial as a central component of dependency and be cautious in relying totally on self-reports by parents or other family members.

An accurate assessment of risk is possible only when those conducting the assessment are knowledgeable about the factors that place children at risk and are skilled in evaluating these factors within the cultural context of the child and family. Accurate risk assessments for chemically involved families are jeopardized by several interrelated factors. The dramatic increase in CPS referrals, combined with budget constraints, has resulted in caseloads far exceeding recommended standards, leaving workers with insufficient time to conduct a thorough assessment. Determinations of risk are further complicated by the inadequate preparation provided to many professionals responsible for conducting CPS assessments. As a result, workers may be unable to assess the level of chemical involvement and the degree of impairment in parenting related to the chemical use.

The bizarre and unpredictable behavior exhibited by many heavily drug-involved parents may also directly jeopardize the assessment. CPS workers and other professionals must confront their own personal feelings toward parents who abuse alcohol or other drugs. Strong negative feelings about alcohol or drugs may cloud the worker's judgment and negatively bias the assessment outcome. On the other hand, personal experiences with alcohol or drugs or more permissive attitudes may cause workers to identify with parents and be overly optimistic about their current level of functioning.

Service Needs Assessment for Alcohol- or Drug-Exposed Infants

Child welfare and health providers are being called upon to assess the needs of chemically exposed infants and to design appropriate interventions to meet their needs. The explosion in the number of infant referrals, combined with the difficulty of the cases, is stressing the child welfare and health care systems and making collaborative efforts more critical. Accurate assessments and services to address identified needs could minimize or reverse negative consequences for these vulnerable children.

When an alcohol- or drug-exposed newborn is discovered in the hospital or reported to child welfare, the response will depend on a variety of factors, including the ability of multiple systems to respond in an appropriate, coordinated, and timely manner. The hospital/medical community must have clearly established policies and procedures for determining that a referral is indicated. The agency charged with responding to the referral must act expeditiously, and the court responsible for deciding whether to separate a child from his/her parents must have adequate information and resources available to act in the best interests of the child and fulfill the requirements of the law.

Regardless of the degree of impairment that an infant or child may have experienced as a result of parental chemical dependency, the challenge is to develop methods of identification, assessment, and intervention to minimize the later damaging effects. These children and their families must be assessed from a holistic perspective and appropriate early intervention services must be provided. It is important to note, however, that at present, when a known alcohol- or drug-exposed infant, toddler, or child comes to the attention of child welfare, the long-term impact of prenatal drug exposure, the effect on the child's development, and his or her developmental potential cannot be predicted with any certainty.

Making Assessments Related to In-Home Services or Placement in Out-of-Home Care

In working with chemically dependent parents, it is the responsibility and duty of child welfare professionals to assess the extent to which parental chemical dependency poses an imminent danger to the child and to determine whether placement away from parents is necessary to assure the child's safety.

The use of alcohol and other drugs is certainly one risk factor that must be assessed. Before taking any action, however, child welfare professionals must assess the use of chemicals in the larger context of family functioning, the availability of community resources, the degree of formal and informal supports, the parents' desire and capacity to parent, the child's attachment and connection to the family, and the likelihood that the child can be kept safe in the home while risk factors are being reduced.

Assessing whether a child needs to be separated from chemically dependent parents requires an understanding of the widely variable effects of alcohol and other drugs, and combinations of drugs, on an adult's ability to parent. Decisions must be made on an individual basis, and the use of a chemical should not be the sole cause of placement. If the family exhibits a desire to remain together, is willing and able to access the services required to pursue sobriety, and has kin or other caregivers willing to assume primary parenting and protection responsibilities until the chemical dependency is addressed, every effort should be extended to foster the parent/child bond and support the family.

In some families, chemical dependency may have eroded both the desire and the ability to parent, and the decision to place the child is clear-cut. In other cases, the parent may voluntarily place the child in family foster care or kinship care. However, in the majority of cases, workers and the courts must make decisions about families who have serious issues to address, including chemical dependency and child maltreatment, as well as existing and potential strengths. In all but a few cases, the parent will express a desire to retain custody of the child, and the decision will have to be made on the basis of the child's safety and well-being.

If the family assessment indicates that the child's safety can be assured by the provision of in-home support or family preservation services, these services must be made available to prevent unnecessary separation of children from their parents. In-home efforts with chemically dependent families are currently in their infancy. The success of the services depends on the ability to accurately evaluate the level of impairment related to alcohol and drug use and to ensure the child's safety while services are provided. Workers must be trained and adequately supported to tailor responses to the unique needs of each chemically dependent family or child. Professionals providing in-home support services must be committed to assisting parents in addressing problems with alcohol or other drugs.

If the family assessment indicates that placement is required, the child welfare agency must assess the child's needs and attempt to find the most appropriate placement option—kinship care, family foster care, or group or residential care. The child's response to placement and the parent's ability to remedy the conditions that led to placement must be continuously monitored and adjustments made on the basis of the ongoing assessment. Too often, assessments are not performed in a timely manner, children and families are not provided with the most appropriate services, and parents are unable to address identified problems due to inadequate community resources.

Judicial Assessments

Juvenile and family court judges must determine whether child welfare agencies have made the reasonable efforts required by P.L. 96-272. This requires assessments at various stages. Before children are placed in out-of-home care, judges must assess whether reasonable efforts have been made to prevent the placement and whether the proposed placement setting is appropriate. In subsequent hearings, the court must assess the status of the child in care and the progress towards reunification or other plans for permanency.

At each stage, the quality of the decisions made is directly related to the quality of the information available to the courts. Information should be provided on the family's strengths and needs, the availability of appropriate services to address those needs, the result of past and present interventions, the willingness and capacity to parent, and the needs and desires of the child.

Once a child has been placed in out-of-home care, an administrative review of the case must occur at least every six months. The court, agency staff, or review boards of citizens may be involved in these periodic reviews, depending on the jurisdiction. In addition to these reviews, a judicial disposition hearing must be held no later than 18 months after the child is initially placed in out-of-home care and periodically thereafter. Too often, particularly in the case of judicial hearings, there is inadequate time allotted or information available to accurately assess the child's or family's status, the agency's efforts toward reunification, or the feasibility of the long-term plan for the child. The purpose of the administrative review, according to federal law, is to determine the continuing necessity for and appropriateness of the placement, the extent of compliance with the case plan, and the extent of progress that has been made toward alleviating or mitigating the causes that led to placement in foster care, and to project a likely date by which the child may be returned home or placed for adoption or legal guardianship.

Federal regulations allow states to define the "periodically thereafter" requirement associated with judicial disposition hearings after the initial 18-month hearing. The purpose of the court review is to determine the future status of the child, including, but not limited to, whether the child should be returned to the parent, should be continued in foster care for a specified period, should be placed for adoption, or should (because of the child's special needs or circumstances) be continued in kinship care or family foster care on a permanent or long-term basis. In the case of a child who has attained age 16, the court reviews services needed to assist the child in making the transition from foster care to independent living.

Alcohol and Drug Assessments

The goal or objective of an intervention determines to a large extent what should be assessed. Alcohol and drug treatment programs have traditionally focused their efforts on the chemically dependent individual with the goal of achieving abstinence. As a result, minimal attention has been given to assessing the individual's functioning within the broader contexts of the family and the community. As an example, the most widely used clinical assessment instrument, the Addiction Severity Index (ASI), devotes only part of one item out of a total of 123 to assessing problems between the individual user and his/her children.[9] Lack of attention to parenting issues is also attributable to the traditional focus on the male as the recipient of addiction treatment.

With the recent phenomenon of crack cocaine abuse among pregnant and parenting women, treatment and child welfare providers are beginning to recognize that they must assess not only addiction, but also the other service needs of the user, the child, and the parent/child dyad. Treatment and service providers are also reviewing the fit between traditional alcohol or drug assessments and the specific issues experienced by pregnant women and parents.

Public Health Assessments

The public health system delivers services designed to promote the health of each community and to reduce the incidence of conditions that cause premature death or disability. Public health and medical providers are often the first to encounter children and families with alcohol or drug problems, especially in the case of infants born exposed to alcohol and other drugs.

Medical providers are currently relying heavily on urine toxicology screens, testing the mother prior to or at the time of birth and/or the infant after birth. A toxicology screen, however, will not be sufficient to assess the needs of the child or the family or the potential risk to the child. Medical and public health professionals must develop a protocol to assess risk and identify the service needs of infants and their families. The assessment should consider risk factors for the infant or child as well as the service needs of the mother.

The public health assessment must address the widely varying needs of alcohol or drug users in different stages or degrees of use or dependence. On the basis of a thorough assessment, the community's public health system must offer prevention, education, and early intervention services to the identified user and to others in the family. Community services should be identified with ongoing efforts to establish and maintain contacts with agencies providing the array of family support and child development and health services.

Developmental Assessments

There appears to be wide variation in the effects of prenatal drug exposure on children, due in large measure to the postnatal environment and the availability of services and interventions to maximize developmental status. Early assessment and intervention services could be generated by an authorized federal program that supports early intervention services for infants and toddlers with developmental delays. Unfortunately, these programs are not uniformly in place and are not available to all or even most families with drug-exposed infants.

P.L. 99-457, also known as the Early Intervention Program of the Individuals with Disabilities Education Act (IDEA), was passed in 1986 to assist the states in establishing a statewide, comprehensive, coordinated, multidisciplinary, interagency system to provide early intervention services for infants and toddlers with developmental delays and their families. Under Part H of IDEA, the states have developed an interagency coordinating council to oversee the development of the system. Federal funding for Part H is limited, and is intended to finance planning and coordination activities; state and local revenues must pay for the actual service delivery. Because some states have encountered significant fiscal problems, they have not moved forward with full program implementation.

Drug-exposed children—even if they begin life under the protection of child welfare services—may well fall into the developmental chasm between the neonatal intensive care unit and Head Start.[10] Current child welfare services for this population do not ensure appropriate developmental assessments or interventions.

Assessments of High-Risk Youth for Chemical Involvement

All too often, the various systems in contact with high-risk youths fail to make an early identification of an alcohol or drug problem. If a problem is identified, little effort is made to thoroughly assess its severity or its relationship with other problems, or to match the problem to the right service. Instead, referral to treatment is often haphazard and arbitrary.

If the assessment is not sensitive to addiction, and the

program does not have an integral prevention, intervention, and treatment focus, an adolescent could be known to child welfare or even remain in care for an extended time without ever addressing a primary condition that jeopardizes his or her life.

Working to Preserve Families

The child welfare system must provide the support that families need to remain together. Services to strengthen and preserve families are critical for supporting children who are at risk because of their parents' use of alcohol or other drugs. When provided with intensive services and support, parents can become motivated to address their drug problems and parent/ child attachment can be fostered.

According to family preservation advocates, successful in-home programs that offer multidisciplinary services are appropriate for chemically dependent families under certain conditions: (1) the program must first correctly identify appropriate families; i.e., those who are motivated to care for the child and willing and able to comply with service plans to ensure protection of the child; (2) the program must be realistic about the existing level of maternal or parental functioning; (3) there must be a long-term commitment to and from the families of sufficient duration to effect change; (4) the program must work with all family members; and (5) consistent funding streams must be available.[11] In some in-home family preservation programs, family maintenance has been enhanced by relocating families out of communities ravaged by drugs and by accessing funds for the families' emergency needs.

Home visiting, as an early intervention strategy, has been shown to be effective in protecting children from serious harm and preventing unnecessary out-of-home placement. These programs have been most effective when there is an appropriate program design and goals are narrowly defined.[12]

Some programs to strengthen and support families have explored the use of legal mandates in their work with actively drug-involved parents. These programs involve mandatory intervention by the courts in cases where a child may be in imminent danger. Courts may order periodic appointments at public health clinics for the child or entry into alcohol or drug treatment programs for the parents. Various services, provided under court supervision, can assist in monitoring child safety and well-being. Mandates in the absence of services, however, are useless in protecting children or strengthening families.

Some family preservation programs also use random drug screens to monitor drug use. This practice remains controversial in the field. If screens are used, a positive toxicology should not result in punitive action or termination of services. Drug testing should not be used in isolation. It should be seen as complementary to and part of therapeutic, ongoing services to strengthen families and assist the chemically involved individual in pursuing recovery.

Of critical importance in the provision of intensive in-home services are the criteria used for selecting families. Families who refuse treatment and are not committed to maintaining the child in the home are not appropriate for these services. Other criteria must also be developed to ensure that the risk to the child is continually monitored while services are being provided. Program design must also be adapted to reflect the chronic nature of addiction and, in some cases, the presence of AIDS or HIV infection, a factor that may necessitate special training for workers providing in-home services.

The intent of short-term, intensive family preservation services is to structure the environment for the safety of the child and not to resolve chronic problems of a family struggling with chemical dependency. However, attention must be given to assuring that families are connected to long-term treatment services in the community in order to sustain gains made during the intensive stages of the intervention.

Additionally, all in-home efforts must be grounded on solid knowledge of the nature of addiction and the need to anticipate and plan for relapse in order to assure the child's safety. Finally, family preservation programs must be appropriately evaluated. The outcome criterion most frequently used to determine success, namely, avoiding placement of the child, is insufficient and inappropriate. Labeling an intervention that results in separation of the child as a "failure" sends the wrong message to the worker, to the family, and especially, to the child.

Making Placement Decisions

Whenever possible, parents need to be free of government interference in the raising of their children. However, society is obligated to protect children from abuse or neglect and to provide them with loving, consistent caregivers when parents cannot or will not assume their parenting roles. Balancing parental rights with the rights and needs of children is always difficult. Chemical dependency further complicates decision making.

In deciding whether to separate a child from a chemically dependent parent, child protective services and the courts must weigh conflicting issues and choose the least damaging alternative for the child. Child welfare professionals and the courts must recognize that relationships with family members are extremely important to a child. Separation from parents, even when they are abusive, neglectful, or chemically dependent, is traumatic for a child and should be avoided whenever possible. If, however, the child is at risk of maltreatment or harm, even with the provision of appropriate family support services, other alternatives must be utilized.

Placement decisions must take into account the unique developmental and emotional needs of the infants, children, and youths requiring out-of-home care. All out-of-home placements should ensure an environment and a system of caregiving that not only meet the basic needs of all children, but also address the unique social and emotional needs of an individual child.

Because of the difficulties children of chemically dependent parents may have in forming attachments and developing interaction skills and appropriate emotional ranges, stable placements with relatives, foster parents, adoptive parents, or other caregivers are imperative. In the case of adolescents who have limited opportunities for reunification or adoption, regardless of placement setting, services must assist in the passage to adulthood and independent living.

Developing Creative Placement Options

The child welfare system generally deals with absolutes. Children either live in their own homes or they are separated from their families and placed in out-of-home care. The reality of practice and placement decisions with today's chemically dependent families offers new opportunities for fostering parent/child connections in ways that challenge traditional thinking.

Consider the following examples:

- The most effective intervention for the chronic, heavily drug-involved mother may be long-term residential drug treatment designed to address multiple needs that are directly and indirectly related to her addiction. The child welfare system supports the practice of allowing children to remain with their mothers in order to foster the mother/child attachment and prevent the trauma associated with separation. In a few programs there is latitude to accommodate this practice. Children reside in residential drug treatment facilities, and for extended periods of the day they are cared for by people other than their parents. They may also receive therapeutic services to meet their physical, mental health, and developmental needs. These children are, in fact, in an out-of-home care setting where they and their mothers receive intensive family support services that are usually provided in the home.

- Increasing numbers of children—as many as half of all foster care children in some jurisdictions—are being placed with relatives who are reimbursed as foster parents. The child is out of his/her home but is still living with "family." This is neither a traditional out-of-home placement nor a family support option, but it may be the best of both worlds, allowing the child to be protected from potential maltreatment while assuring increased placement stability and ongoing connection to the family.

- In some communities, twenty-four hour crisis nurseries or therapeutic shelter programs provide emergency out-of-home care services for infants and young children who need immediate protection. Children may remain for days, weeks, or months in these programs. Clearly, these are out-of-home care placements. However, many of these centers also actively strive to develop a relationship with parents and to serve as an ongoing support center for the child and the family long after the child is returned home. This is one example of how an out-of-home care placement can also become an ongoing center of support for families. In fact, the availability of and connection to a crisis center is often the critical factor that allows parents who are chemically dependent to manage their children safely. They learn to turn to the center before neglecting or abusing their children and before relapsing. In essence, a center can be as effective as having a family support worker available twenty-four hours a day.

Other examples of creativity in placement options and practices are emerging. There are now a few programs that place whole families in host/foster family homes, thereby allowing children to be supported by their own families. There are renewed efforts to empower community mentors to serve as long-term family support workers. These volunteers are trained and assisted to provide case management and support to chemically involved families living in their own communities. Volunteers may be perceived more positively than outside "experts," and when relapse occurs, children remain connected to a family and neighborhood friend.

All of these options realistically address the needs of children and their chemically involved families. The challenge is for the child welfare system, as a whole, to continue to build on and expand creative placement alternatives.

Providing Quality Out-of-Home Care

Parental chemical dependency and out-of-home care placements are directly related. The increase in alcohol- and other drug-related CPS referrals and the lack of community alcohol and drug resources and family support services have resulted in more children needing out-of-home care. The increases are occurring in communities hard hit by the drug epidemic. According to data collected by the American Public Welfare Association, the five states with the largest number of children in foster care in FY 1989 (California, New York, Illinois, Pennsylvania, and Ohio) had 47% of the nation's total foster care population.[13] Ten percent of all children in care reside in New York City.[14]

Children are remaining in foster care for longer periods of time. These lengthy stays may deprive children of a sense of belonging. In addition, the longer the stay, the more likely it is that the child will be subjected to multiple placements—each of which can prove as devastating as the initial separation from parents. These current foster care statistics are particularly sobering:

- Infants, toddlers, and preschoolers are the fastest growing foster care population. In 1980, only 19% of all foster children were under age five.[15] Today, in some cities, almost half of the children in care are under five.[16]

- One in three foster care admissions in New York City is a child under two years old.[17] In New York State the rates of infant placement rose from 6.5/1,000 in 1986 to 11.4/1,000 in 1987 and 15.6/1,000 in 1988. Illinois saw an increase from 3.4/1,000 in 1986 to 5/1,000 in 1988.[18]

- Fewer than 40% of children under 10 who remain in out-of-home care longer than 18 months will ever return home. The rate may be as low as 10 to 20% in cases of chemically dependent parents. Unless adoption or legal guardianship becomes an option, they are likely to move from one placement to another.[19]

- In a Harlem hospital study of 1,900 cocaine-exposed babies, only 25% of the polydrug-using mothers were caring for their babies. The majority were cared for by grandmothers.[20]

- Children of substance abusers remain in out-of-home care longer than other children. Sixty percent of babies discharged from the hospital to foster care were still there three years later.[21]

- In addition to the increasing time spent in out-of-home care, children are also faced with increasing numbers of disrupted placements. Of children in foster care, 23.2% will have two placements, 20.1% will have three to five placements, and 6.9% will have six or more placements.[22]

Family Foster Care Challenges for Infants and Young Children

In the absence of a national, effective intervention and prevention strategy to eliminate or reduce chemical dependency and the host of problems it engenders for children, the child welfare system must be prepared to address the long-term needs of drug-exposed children or children of substance abusers (COSAs) through its various services. In spite of the best intentions, certain aspects of the system may negatively impact on a child's ability to form a significant attachment or maximize developmental potential.

Overwhelmed foster parents, overcrowded/understaffed residential or group homes, multiple placements, and the separation of siblings can only compound the risks to the child. While the system strives to place infants and young children "temporarily" with consistent, responsive, loving caretakers, regardless of the setting, until reunification or relinquishment takes place, this is often far from reality. The shortage of foster parents trained and supported to accept infants, and in particular, special-needs infants, has resulted in placing more children in each available home, in the shifting of children from one home to another, and in the frequent separation of siblings. Low reimbursement rates are the most commonly cited explanation for the shortage of foster parents. Many foster parents have not qualified for higher reimbursement because at the time of placement, the infants or young children did not appear to require specialized care. When the real needs and expenses of providing care become apparent, the system does not adequately support the caregivers.

In addition to the financial drain, foster parents also cite lack of training and support services—such as child day care, respite care, transportation, and access to health and mental health services—as reasons for not accepting or keeping these challenging infants and young children.[23]

Some communities have acknowledged the difficulty of

caring for medically fragile and/or challenging children and their families in traditional foster homes, and have developed specialized homes with highly trained parents, operating in partnership with multidisciplinary professional staff. These specialized foster families receive higher reimbursement rates, respite care, and extensive training in the special care of their children. Child welfare professionals are recognizing that what is required of foster parents today is significantly different from what was required a decade ago. Just as the children's needs have changed, so have the expectations the system has for foster families. The intensity of care some children need demands high quality professional service. Professional services are costly. As a result, few communities have an adequate supply of qualified, trained, and well-supported family foster care providers.

Challenges Posed by Kinship Care

The placement of infants or young children of chemically dependent parents with relatives or other members of the kinship network is an option that is receiving increased attention. In some jurisdictions, kinship care placements are mandated as the placement option of choice for children entering care. One of the most dramatic examples of the increased use of kinship care is occurring in New York City. From 1986 to 1991 the kinship care population went from 1,000 to over 20,000, and now accounts for half of the city's children in foster care.[24] In the fall of 1990, the Illinois Department of Children and Family Services reported that 8,347 or 46% of its 18,125 foster children were living in kinship care arrangements, a 12% increase in three years. If the total U.S. foster care population is placed at 400,000, it can be estimated conservatively that more than 100,000 children are living in kinship care arrangements.[25] The increase is generally attributed to a willingness on the part of extended families to care for their relatives when asked to do so, combined with a shortage of non-relative foster parents.

The debate on kinship care is often focused on whether or not families should be paid to care for children of relatives. Levels of reimbursement for kinship care vary from one area to another. Some kinship providers receive AFDC reimbursement. In some cities they are reimbursed as state-approved, licensed family foster care providers and receive foster care reimbursement, which may be insufficient, but is significantly higher than AFDC. In still other states, some kinship providers may not be eligible for AFDC, because in these states, AFDC is limited to "blood relatives." Therefore, godmothers and others in the kinship network do not qualify.

Instead of limiting the discussion to funding for kinship care, attention should be devoted to assessing whether kinship care, over an extended period of time, is a good environment for raising a particular child. If the answer to that question is yes, many child welfare experts believe that adequate funding to support the care should be made available.[26]

The rapid increase in the use of kinship care has caught child welfare agencies unprepared. Local, state, and national efforts are underway to adapt policies and practices to meet the needs of these special foster parents. Unless kinship care programs are evaluated, monitored, and supported, kinship care could lead in some cases to the abuse and neglect of vulnerable children.[27] Because chemical dependency is often intergenerational, and because so many chemically dependent women were physically or sexually abused as children, kinship placements should not be assumed to be safe. Assessment and ongoing monitoring of such placements must be done to ensure the well-being of the child.

Studies are beginning to show that children placed with relatives stay in care longer than those in non-relative placements. The effect of prolonged stays on the child is not known, but these placements tend to be more stable than non-relative placements. Controversy remains in the field over the use of kinship care as a permanent placement option for children.[28]

In some cases, kinship care may be a child's best hope of a permanent family. But if children are to be placed permanently with kin, many of these families may require ongoing support and long-term financial assistance.

Challenges Posed by Residential or Group Care

Conventional practice has dictated that if placement is necessary for infants and young children, a family setting with relative or non-relative caregivers is the preferred placement option. However, the urgent demand for immediate placements for children with very complex needs has exceeded the supply of qualified family foster parents. In addition, the need for immediate, comprehensive child/family assessment and treatment planning and the need for professionally staffed 24-hour intensive services have given rise to new group care concepts for certain alcohol- or drug-exposed infants or other young children requiring this level of care.

Child-centered, family-focused, short-term group or residential care is an essential part of the full array of child welfare services needed for children and youths of all ages. As in any setting, providing individualized care is essential. Given the current state of knowledge about child development and the special needs of children of chemically involved parents, it is critical to design an environment and a system of caregiving that are individualized, nurturing, and able to meet the individual child's needs.

In addition to managing increasing numbers of infants and young children, traditional child welfare group and residential facilities are also struggling to meet the needs of seriously disturbed children and adolescents, especially those for whom drug use is a factor. Older adolescents frequently cannot gain access to an alcohol or drug treatment program that meets their needs, and few child welfare residential treatment programs have been prepared to address substance abuse problems.

As with all other forms of out-of-home care, placement of

a child of any age in residential or group care should never be an excuse for not attempting to engage the family. Residential care programs must overcome difficulties in involving chemically dependent parents in planning and caring for their children. Programs must adapt to the unique needs of medically fragile, AOD-exposed children or children and adolescents with HIV/AIDS. Here, as in all cases, discharges from residential care to kinship care, to family foster care, or to reunification with parents should be planned to minimize the disruption to the child. Older adolescents should receive services to prepare them for independent living when they leave the protective environment of residential or group care.

Planning for Permanency

An assessment of the fit between the requirements of P.L. 96-272 and the needs of a drug-exposed infant or child of chemically dependent parents requires a focus on what will maximize the child's physical, emotional, cognitive, and social development. Such an effort inevitably raises tensions between those who advocate reducing barriers to adoption or other plans to facilitate permanent homes and stable environments for children and those who advocate family reunification.

The overriding determinant must be the child's best interests. The challenge with infants and children of chemically dependent parents is to determine what that means. It is difficult to say with any certainty how long the system should wait for parents to become willing or able to parent their children before implementing an alternative permanent plan.

Anecdotal evidence strongly indicates that chemical dependency plays a significant role in debilitating families and making reunification efforts far more difficult and protracted. Crack and other drugs widely in use today have exacerbated the long-standing problem of meeting the needs of the children of substance abusers. In the 1970s, research studies found that children of alcohol- or drug-involved parents were in foster care longer than any other population, were moved from one placement to another more frequently, and were less likely to return home to their parents. They were more difficult to plan for, in part because of their parents' inability to become active participants in the planning process.[29]

Barriers to Reunification

In a study of 1,003 African American children who entered foster care in five cities, children of chemically involved parents were compared with children who entered care for other reasons. The children of substance abusers who were placed in care were younger, with a median age of 4.7 years compared to 7.5 years for children without parental AOD involvement.

The study reached the following conclusions:

- The child welfare system is not achieving permanency for most children, but especially not when alcohol or drug involvement is a factor. At the end of 26 months, only 28% of the children of chemically involved parents had been discharged from care, as compared to 51% of the other children.

- Child neglect was likely to have been the primary reason for placement of children with chemically involved parents, while child abuse was more likely for other children needing placement.

- Families often did not receive services to address the problems that led to the child's placement. For instance, only 60% of chemically involved parents were even referred for AOD treatment services, and it is likely that far fewer actually received appropriate services.

Many of the service needs identified when children entered care remained as barriers to reunification at the end of the study.[30]

Other studies have identified additional barriers to reunification. Among these barriers:

- When children are in foster care, the child welfare system devotes little effort to preserving and strengthening the parent/child attachment. This is particularly true with chemically involved parents, who may have difficulty keeping regularly scheduled appointments to visit their children. As long as reunification is the goal, the system must find more effective ways to support the relationship during the period of separation.

- The unavailability or ineffectiveness of affordable drug treatment combined with the uneven path of recovery may be the most serious barrier to reunification. Parents may be mandated to receive treatment in order to regain custody of their children. These mandates, however, occur in the absence of appropriate services, and even if parents are able to overcome access barriers, long-term residential treatment may be required. In the meantime, children are experiencing prolonged stays in out-of-home care settings, often developing significant attachments to their caregivers.

- Even when treatment is available, there clearly are no guarantees that a chemically dependent parent will successfully become and remain drug- or alcohol-free. To begin with, there is inadequate information as to what constitutes effective drug treatment for different population groups.[31] For the heavily addicted or chronic daily drug user, traditional treatment models have met with limited success.[32] Studies have shown that even after completing treatment, only about 25% of people dependent on crack cocaine, for example, are able to remain drug free six months after discharge.[33]

Despite the barriers to reunification, the majority of children entering foster care do eventually return to their parents. However, in recent years an increasing number of children have left foster care only to reenter the system later. Between 1983 and 1985, the number of children with multiple placements in foster care rose from 16% to 30%.[34] Recent studies in New York state found that 27% of all children reunited with their families returned to placement some time later; in Illinois, the comparable figure is 30%.[35] Too frequently, appropriate reunification and aftercare services are not provided to prevent reentry.

Termination of Parental Rights

As a result of the difficulty in reuniting children with their chemically involved parents, some have urged a reexamination of termination of parental rights procedures. The child welfare system and the courts are confronted daily with the reality that what may be in the best interests of a child may conflict with the desires of some chemically dependent parents, who refuse to relinquish the right to parent but lack the ability to do so.

Termination of parental rights entails a legal finding that parental rights and responsibilities for a child should be permanently severed. Termination removes a parent's right to regain custody of the child regardless of how the situation may change. The criteria for termination are defined under state laws, with wide variability among states. Grounds are usually based on some pattern of parental conduct or condition that is not amenable to successful intervention and that makes the parents unable to parent a child. Being chemically dependent is now included in a number of statutes as one of the grounds for termination of parental rights.[36]

In addition to finding the parent unable to parent, the court must also determine that termination is in the child's best interests. The primary reason for termination is to allow a child to be adopted when reunification is not possible. In almost all states, the decision to initiate termination is left to the discretion of child welfare agencies.

Whenever newspaper headlines describe infants abandoned or children repeatedly endangered by chemically dependent parents, child welfare agencies' termination procedures are scrutinized. On the one hand, efforts to proceed quickly are criticized for failing to try hard enough to reunite families by providing appropriate services and supports. Should a mother's right to raise her child be terminated when she has never received access to drug treatment to remedy the condition that necessitated placement? On the other hand, when child welfare agencies do not aggressively pursue termination, critics argue that the system is insensitive to the developmental needs of the child and her or his right to a permanent, safe, loving family.

Over the past decade, research has been conducted to determine factors that reduce the length of time spent in foster care and the timely achievement of permanent placements. Early case planning, reduced caseload size, written contracts, intensified casework services with parents, and frequent parental contact appear to contribute to successful, timely implementation of the permanency plan.[37]

The child welfare system must clearly outline the specific efforts that should be undertaken to reunite families and the point at which a child is entitled to a permanent home apart from his or her biological family. Such an effort requires clarification of the legal meanings of "abandonment," "reunification," and "reasonable efforts to reunite families," and mandates the establishment of rational, enforceable legal decision points at which a permanent plan will be made.[38] The child welfare system cannot do this alone. The legal, political, alcohol and drug treatment, and social services delivery systems must work with the child welfare system to respond to the problems of chemically dependent families.

Planning for Adoption, Independence, and Aftercare

Adoption as a Permanency Option

The increased use of adoption for children unlikely to be reunited with their parents presents one opportunity to prevent long-term stays in foster care. A number of studies have shown that the likelihood of reunification decreases over time—that is, the longer a child remains in foster care, the less likely it is that he or she will return home.[39] The time after which reunification becomes unlikely has been alternately placed at 18 months,[40] six months,[41] and 10 weeks.[42] Yet, children who are adopted have typically remained in foster care for three to five years before the adoption.[43] Some states are considering ways to speed up the adoption process.

In fact, unlike other areas of child welfare practice, adoption services have not been dramatically impacted by the drug epidemic. Child welfare agencies have been reluctant to give up on biological parents who have had few opportunities to remedy their chemical dependency problems. In addition, many agencies erroneously assume that children with special needs are "unadoptable," and therefore do not aggressively recruit adoptive parents for these children.

There are other barriers. For example, in the case of drug-exposed infants, prospective adoptive parents may be anxious about the long-term effects of the exposure and the possible need for expensive medical, educational, and psychological care. In other cases, child welfare agencies have not successfully recruited same-race, same-culture adoptive parents.

In the absence of suitable adoptive parents, or policies and practices to support them, questions arise about the ethics of termination proceedings. Is it ethical to sever the legal ties and responsibilities of biological parents when, as happens too frequently, children freed for adoption may remain indefinitely in the foster care system?

Removing Barriers to Adoption

If adoption is to become a viable option for large numbers of alcohol- or drug-exposed children, massive efforts will be required to recruit, train, and support sufficient numbers of same-race, same-culture adoptive parents. Post-adoptive services will have to be significantly enhanced to support large numbers of adoptive parents who are willing and able to accept the challenges that a child with special needs may create. Some cities and states are already experiencing a lack of adoptive parents for children with special needs. Drug-exposed, possibly HIV-positive children may need intensive levels of services and care for an indefinite time.

It will also be necessary to promote adoption as a viable option for children who cannot be reunited with parents. The goal of permanency through either reunification or adoption is ultimately met for about two-thirds of the children in foster care. Currently, only about 7% are adopted.[44]

One proposed permanency solution is to place children from families who seem unlikely to be able to parent them again with foster parents who are also prepared to become adoptive parents. These foster families can be screened and trained to parent a special-needs infant or child with the understanding that if parental rights are terminated, they will proceed with the adoption. If reunification remains the goal, the foster parents agree to accept and support that decision.

Independence for Adolescents

Older adolescents in the foster care system who will not be reunited with parents are entitled to services to prepare them for independence. These services are not sufficiently available or adequate in scope to help even a fraction of the young adults who could benefit.

It is ironic that the resources to support these services are unavailable to 18- to-21-year-olds leaving foster care when even middle class, well-educated young people from stable family environments are returning home after failing to achieve independence in these hard economic times. Young adults who are exiting foster care, still carrying the scars preceding and resulting from placement, may require additional services if they are going to safely make the transition to independence. Clear evidence of this is the fact that many of our young homeless people were in the foster care system before failing at independence, ending up on the streets, and trying to find a bed in a different shelter each day.

Supporting Permanency for Chemically Dependent Families

Foster care is supposed to be a stable, nurturing temporary stopover on the way to a permanent home. A glance at the statistics demonstrates that placement in foster care is seldom temporary, however, while "permanence" is becoming an elusive goal. Specifically with regard to chemical dependence, permanence is an unworkable and unrealistic demand.

As a chemically dependent parent develops insight into addiction and the recovery process begins, she or he becomes aware that "clean and sober" is not a permanent condition but a daily commitment. This recognition constitutes real progress in recovery, and can be helpful in making "permanent" plans for the child with a parent whose recovery status may fluctuate.

This reality does not mean abandoning goals of permanency through reunification, adoption, or independence; it may, however, mean rethinking how the system can best support the goal of permanency when the child is reunited with a chemically dependent parent. Families are too often reunited during a brief moment of sobriety and then left alone with minimal services or supports. Children may be reunited with parents only to reenter foster care within weeks or months.

Child welfare and other child and family agencies should assure that chemically dependent parents who are reunited with their children receive help to continue their recovery and to prepare for the care and protection of their children if a relapse should occur. Efforts should be made to phase in the return of the children and to provide the family ongoing support and aftercare. Ongoing relationships with foster parents or community child and family support centers may help with the adjustments.

In permanency planning, greater emphasis needs to be placed on providing consistent and caring people to meet children's needs today, tomorrow, and the day after. If the parent is chemically dependent, he or she may not be able to meet the child's day-to-day needs unless provided with long-term supports. In the case of chemically dependent families, this requires accepting from the beginning that the family, by virtue of the lifelong nature of the condition, will require variable levels of support on a permanent basis. Child welfare agencies should place an emphasis on developing formal and informal networks—relatives or kin, neighbors, agencies, or host families—from the time the family is referred, through the recovery process, and continuing as a resource for the child during times of relapse or when residential drug treatment is needed. Children may still need to be placed in out-of-home care from time to time, but in these cases the child could be placed with someone from the family's network. If reunification is the goal, the family could be supported immediately by the mobilized community upon the child's return home.

The brevity of most family support or intensive family preservation services is not consistent with the reality that drug treatment for many chemically dependent individuals may require a year or two and that recovery is a lifelong process characterized by the potential for recurring periods of relapse. In-home preservation services are often initiated when the family is in acute crisis and discontinued when the family can most benefit from support, at the front end of recovery and/or after reunification with the child. Short-term crisis services are vital and must be available. However, these acute, time-limited services should be supplemented by an array of other services to strengthen and support chemically dependent families on a long-term basis. If families are not provided ongoing support, they may not be able to sustain gains made in treatment, and too often their children will reenter the child welfare system.

In summary, regardless of the permanency option sought—reunification, adoption, guardianship, or independence—it is essential to recognize that children and families will need additional services or supports from time to time so placements intended to last a lifetime can be successful. It is critical that services to strengthen families be provided when children return home following placement. Biological parents and adoptive parents must receive an array of services and supports to assure that children remain in loving, stable families. And, finally, increased effort must go into supporting young adults to be able to reach their full potential after leaving the foster care system.

Addressing Broader Issues

The child welfare system, as part of its mission to protect and support the well-being of children, must recognize the role that larger social forces play in the quality of children's lives. The child welfare system does not exist in a vacuum but interacts and often overlaps with other service delivery systems that can positively or negatively impact the welfare of children. To achieve the overriding goal of enhancing the quality of children's lives, the child welfare system must help to identify and rectify social conditions that negatively affect children.

It is critical for all providers to recognize that chemical dependency is only one of many serious and long-standing problems confronting families who come to the attention of the child welfare system. When chemical dependency occurs in families coping with problems of poverty, substandard housing and homelessness, the absence of community and family support services, and pervasive feelings of alienation and hopelessness, the negative impact on children and on overall family functioning will be significantly increased. Chemical dependency adds to the sense of powerlessness and social isolation felt by many parents and children in the child welfare system.

Child welfare professionals must recognize and address the multiple factors that place children and families at risk. Families must be supported in building on their inherent strengths. The child welfare system must advocate for social policies to meet the basic needs of families and make them less vulnerable to problems with alcohol and other drugs.

Endnotes

1. The National Committee for the Prevention of Child Abuse (NCPCA), "The Results of the 50-State Annual Surveys," Chicago, IL: NCPCA 1991.

2. NCPCA 1991.

3. NCPCA 1991.

4. Child Welfare League of America, *Standards for Services for Abused or Neglected Children and Their Families*, Washington, DC: The Child Welfare League of America, 1989.

5. Herkowitz, J.; Seck, M.; and Fogg, C., "Substance Abuse and Family Violence: Identification of Drug and Alcohol Usage During Child Abuse Investigations," Boston, MA: Department of Social Studies, 1989.

6. NCPCA 1991.

7. National Commission on Children, *Beyond Rhetoric*, Washington, DC: National Commission on Children, 1991, 284.

8. U.S. Department of Health and Human Services (DHHS), National Institute of Mental Health, "Provisional Estimate of Census Data," Statistical Research Branch, Division of Applied and Services Research, unpublished data, 1988. Cited in *Beyond Rhetoric*, 284.

9. Schottenfeld, R.S., "Treatment Programs and Prognosis," Paper presented at the American Enterprise Institute Conference, July 1991.

10. Barth, Richard P., "Protecting Children of Heavy Drug Users: A Call for Sustained Protection and Prevention Services," Paper presented at the American Enterprise Institute Conference, July 1991.

11. West, Kathleen, Presentation at the Child Welfare League of America Symposium "Crack and Other Addictions," March 1990.

12. U.S. General Accounting Office, "Home Visiting: A Promising Early Intervention Strategy for High-Risk Families," Washington, DC: GAO, July 1990.

13. Tatara, Toshio, "Children of Substance Abusing/Alcoholic Parents Referred to the Public Child Welfare System, Summaries of Key Statistical Data Obtained from States," Washington, DC: American Public Welfare Association, n.d.

14. Sabol, Barbara J., Testimony to U.S. House of Representatives Subcommittee on Human Resources, Ways and Means Committee, April 30, 1991.

15. Mangano, Michael, Testimony to the U.S. Senate Labor and Human Resources Committee, Subcommittee on Children, Families, Drugs and Alcohol, March 8, 1990. Testimony based upon State of New York Senate Committee on Investigations, Taxation and Government Operations, "Crack Babies: The Shame of New York," December 1989: 4.

16. Mangano 1990.

17. Sabol 1991.

18. Wulcyzn, F., and Goerge, R., Data presented at Child Welfare Symposium on Multi-State Foster Care, New York, May 1991.

19. Wald, Michael, "Termination of Parental Rights," Paper presented at the American Enterprise Institute Conference (AEI), July 1991.

20. Davis, Evelyn, Testimony before the U.S. House of Representatives Select Committees on Narcotics Abuse and Control, July 30, 1991.

21. Besharov, D.J., "The Children of Crack: Will We Protect Them?," *Public Welfare* 47, 4 (Fall 1989): 6–11.

22. Tatara, Toshio, "Characteristics of Children in Substitute and Adoptive Care: A Statistical Summary of the VCIS National Child Welfare Data Base," Washington, DC: American Public Welfare Association, July 1991.

23. U.S. Department of Health and Human Services (DHHS), Office of the Inspector General, "Crack Babies," Washington DC: U.S. Government Printing Office, February 1990, 9.

24. Sabol 1991.

25. Curtis, P., Testimony: "A Research Agenda for Child Abuse and Neglect," National Research Council, Commission on Behavioral and Social Sciences and Education, January 8, 1992.

26. Johnson, Ivory, "Kinship Care: Preserving Families," Paper presented at the American Enterprise Institute Conference, July 1991.

27. Johnson 1991.

28. Johnson 1991.

29. Fanshel, David, "Parental Failure and Consequences for Children: The Drug Abusing Mother Whose Children are in Foster Care," *American Journal of Public Health* 65, 6 (June 1975): 604–612.

30. National Black Child Development Institute, "Parental Drug Abuse and African American Children in Foster Care, Issues and Study Findings," Prepared under a contract to the Assistant Secretary for Planning and Evaluation, U.S. Department of Health and Human Services, Washington, DC, February 1991.

31. U.S. General Accounting Office, "Drug Abuse: Research on Treatment May Not Address Current Needs," Washington, DC: Government Printing Office, September 1990.

32. Besharov 1989.

33. Koppelman, J., and Jones, J., "Crack: It is Destroying Low-Income Families," *Public Welfare* 47, 4 (Fall 1989): 13–15.

34. U.S. House of Representatives Select Committee on Children, Youth and Families, "No Place to Call Home," Washington, DC: Government Printing Office, 1989, 19.

35. Goerge, R., and Wulcyzn, F. "Placement Duration and Foster Care Re-entry in New York and Illinois: A Discussion Paper," Chicago, IL: Chapin Hall, 1990, 31.

36. Wald 1991.

37. Katz, Linda, "Effective Permanency Planning for Children in Foster Care," Washington, DC: National Association of Social Workers, 1990.

38. Kroll, J., Testimony before the U.S. Senate Committee on Labor and Human Resources Subcommittee on Children, Family, Drugs and Alcohol, March 8, 1990.

39. Kroll 1990.

40. Goerge, R., "The Reunification Process in Foster Care," in *Social Service Review* 64, 3 (September 1990): 422–457.

41. Maas, H., and Engler, R., *Children in Need of Parents*, New York: Columbia University Press, 1989.

42. New York City Comptroller General, "Whatever Happened to the Boarder Babies?" A report by the Comptroller General, New York, 1988.

43. Goerge 1990.

44. U.S. Department of Health and Human Services, Office of the Inspector General, "Barriers to Freeing Children for Adoption," Washington, DC: DHHS, February 1991.

5

Overview of the Challenges to Related Systems

The child welfare system is only one part of the vast network of health and human service agencies providing services to children and families. This chapter will review the current challenges and responses of the alcohol and drug prevention field, the juvenile and family courts, the health care system, Head Start programs, and the schools with regard to today's chemically involved children and families.

Alcohol and Drug Abuse Prevention and Treatment

The need for vigorous enforcement efforts to combat illegal drugs is clear. Yet there is broad agreement that the best hope for reducing the demand for drugs of all kinds, including alcohol, is through prevention and treatment efforts.

—*The National Association of State Alcohol and Drug Abuse Directors*

The alcohol and drug treatment field has historically been far removed from child welfare. Until recently, most drug treatment programs were targeted toward adult males, with only minimal attention paid to the needs of their families or children. Traditional adult residential programs have always excluded children, and even outpatient services have paid little attention to the needs of women or women with children. There has been only minimal interest in addressing the special needs of the adolescent alcohol or drug user, who may have complex needs in addition to the issues related to chemical use.

Service providers frequently have little understanding of each other's fields, despite the reality that chemical dependency treatment programs routinely treat victims and perpetrators of child abuse or maltreatment, and child welfare agencies frequently deal with chemically dependent families when they intervene to protect a child. Alcohol and drug treatment professionals often do not inquire about parenting behavior, child abuse and neglect, or other risks to the child in the home. Failure to inquire may be based on a professional preference for not knowing. In a survey of alcohol and drug therapists, almost 40% expressed concern that reporting suspected abuse would harm their relationships with patients.[1] Similarly, child welfare workers have not been educated to understand chemical dependency and its impact on family functioning. Too often, they have not been trained to ask about or respond to AOD issues.

The dramatic increase in AOD use among women of childbearing years, however, has caused a shift. It has brought about a recognition of the urgent need to adapt existing AOD prevention and treatment programs to respond to the needs of women and children and the urgent need for child welfare professionals to develop expertise in AOD issues.

Scope of the Problem

Despite the overwhelming need for these services, AOD abuse prevention and treatment are not readily available. For example:

- The city of New York has 200,000 intravenous drug users (half of them HIV positive) and only 38,000 publicly-funded treatment slots.[2]

- Nationwide, treatment admissions to publicly funded programs for heroin and cocaine combined increased by over 200% between 1985 and 1990.[3]

- NIDA recently estimated that 107,000 people are on waiting lists for drug treatment.[4] The average wait for a residential program is 45 days.[5]

- Each year, 1.5 million persons receive drug treatment, 123,000 of whom are adolescents. The total number of persons needing treatment in 1989 was estimated to be 10.6 million, including over 1.7 million adolescents.[6]

Funding and Priorities for AOD Treatment Services

Despite recent significant increases, federal spending for AOD treatment services lags far behind state financial commitments. The National Association of State Alcohol and Drug Abuse Directors (NASADAD) reported that for FY90, state governments contributed 47.6% of the total amount spent for treatment and prevention, while the federal government contributed only 29%. Since state and local governments continue to fund most of the services, and since many communities are in fiscal crisis, the scope and availability of services vary widely. It is often those communities with the greatest needs that have the fewest resources.

With respect to drug-exposed children, the federal government has concentrated its efforts primarily on research and information dissemination regarding drug effects and on funding limited services through block grants to the states or through narrowly defined service demonstration programs. The weakest efforts thus far have been in determining and implementing effective interventions to ameliorate the problems faced by AOD-involved families.[7]

Education, Prevention, and Early Intervention Needs

Prevention efforts, especially for women of childbearing years, must be a national priority, not only in rhetoric but also in the balance of spending priorities. Although it may be possible to reverse some or most of the negative consequences related to prenatal AOD exposure with early intervention and special services, some children will suffer physiological, psychological, or developmental consequences irrespective of the quality or amount of intervention they receive. Prevention services aimed at prenatal care and the prevention of parental drug abuse must be available in order to make a real difference. Efforts should include aggressive outreach and education about the risks of drug use, especially during pregnancy; the importance of prenatal care and good nutrition; and the impact of parental AOD use and abuse on children. Women must have improved access to quality health and human services, and especially to AOD treatment services designed to meet their needs. Effective programs must be based on an understanding of the nature of addiction and the contributing factors that may have preceded AOD use in women. Services must be offered through schools, health clinics, and other institutions that reach young women. Services must be coordinated with successful programs such as WIC, which attracts low-income young women and their families because it provides the nutritional services they need and want. This program could easily be expanded, if sufficient resources were committed, to include AOD education and counseling, early identification, and referral.

A national public education campaign is also needed to bring family alcoholism out of the closet for open discussion and action. The possibility that persons at risk for alcoholism could be identified before they began drinking holds the exciting promise of true primary prevention.

In the past decade, the federal government has embarked on a variety of campaigns to prevent alcohol and drug abuse, investing heavily in "Just Say No" messages to deter initial use by children and adolescents. Policymakers now recognize that "Just Say No" is not enough, and they are beginning to turn their attention to the needs of youths who are already abusing drugs or who are caught up in the drug trade. The Office for Substance Abuse Prevention (OSAP) high-risk youth program is attempting to design and promote culturally sensitive prevention strategies targeted to attract the toughest children and youths, those who are most difficult to dissuade. Efforts similar to OSAP's must be replicated in communities across the country and supported by adequate, stable funding sources. Leadership at the national level must promote and support specific prevention strategies tailored to local community needs, targeting specific populations, with improved outcome data to evaluate each.

Effective Treatment

A 30-day detox program will not put an addict into recovery. The road to recovery is long and full of relapses.

—Judith Burnison
president, NAPARE

All programs should treat addiction as a primary condition that must be addressed while looking at the needs of the total person, including factors contributing to addiction and barriers to recovery. These factors may include poverty, lack of education, lack of job training, and a history of sexual and physical abuse. Programs should be culturally sensitive and provide training in parenting, good nutrition, and navigating the complex health and human services systems.

Most importantly, an effective program does not treat chemical dependency as an individual illness. It is a family affair. As this recognition has spread over the past decade, the family has increasingly been included in all treatment settings.

Programs of all kinds—outreach, outpatient, and residential—
are making great strides in engaging all family members in the
process of recovery.

Another important factor in successful programs is the
recognition that relapse is a part of recovery and should be
expected in the process of AOD treatment. The most common
feature of drug or alcohol abuse is relapse. Because relapse is
to be anticipated, successful programs must have ready responses—pre-planning, supportive services, and resources to
protect children.

Given the variety of treatment approaches, what is known
to work best? At this point, it appears that no treatment
modality is clearly superior to another. After 15 years of studies
on alcohol and drug abuse treatment, the evidence is clear that
treatment of virtually every type is effective to some degree. The
generic question of what works best needs to be replaced by an
effort to establish which treatments are effective for which
individuals at what point in their addictive process. The real
mystery is why so little is spent treating dependency and so
much is spent paying for its effects—crime, violence, family
breakups, poverty, lost production, and lost lives.[8]

Treatment for Adolescents and Women

Until the past decade there were very few alcohol or drug
programs specifically designed for women or adolescents. This
is beginning to change. According to the 1989 survey by the
National Drug and Alcoholism Treatment Unit Survey
(NDATUS), 84.5% of youth clients were treated in a unit
offering a youth program, 664 treatment centers reported that
at least 50% of their clients were youths, and 379 centers
reported that 100% of their clients were youths. Six percent of
alcohol admissions and 15% of drug admissions were adolescents.[9]

The quality and availability of drug treatment for women,
especially for pregnant women, is also improving. According to

the most recent NDATUS survey, 31% of alcohol and drug treatment admissions were women (207,510). Women account for 26% of alcohol clients and 35% of drug clients.[10]

Treatment Capacity

Despite recent improvements in some communities, the demand for multifaceted, comprehensive, culturally responsive, coordinated substance abuse prevention, treatment, and aftercare services for all age groups still far exceeds the supply. The worst problems occur in a few states with large urban centers. For example, New York and California together had 33% of the nation's drug admissions, including 44% of the nation's heroin admissions. New York, California, Florida, Illinois, Massachusetts, and Pennsylvania now account for 48% of all drug treatment admissions, while having 36% of the nation's population.[11]

The large numbers of individuals seeking treatment in relation to scarce treatment resources inevitably creates waiting lists. Waiting lists can have a devastating effect on the system's ability to involve AOD abusers in treatment. At the time treatment is sought, the individual has successfully broken through his or her denial; if required to wait, he or she may no longer be ready, and may even be impossible to find when an opening for treatment develops.

Actions at the federal, state, and local levels, while showing improvement, have not adequately responded to the need for increased services, particularly for pregnant women and women with children. While funding has increased for this population, the need for treatment and related services continues to outpace supply. In response to concerns about treatment capacity there have been calls for "treatment on demand." However, the open-ended expansion of treatment capacity has been criticized at the federal level on several grounds, including the following: (1) available treatment slots often remain unfilled because of poor coordination of treatment waiting lists; (2) not all treatment is of equal effectiveness, and the indiscriminate expansion of treatment slots will not necessarily meet the needs of underserved populations; and (3) treatment on demand may create a revolving door effect, with AOD abusers moving in and out of treatment programs without ever taking treatment seriously.[12]

To effectively provide treatment, coordination is critically needed, but coordination alone will not be sufficient to meet the needs of all who require treatment services. Research is needed to determine what works best with various populations of drug abusers. Treatment models proven to be effective should be expanded and made available to individuals seeking help.

Treatment Needs

At present, there are serious shortages of all types of treatment programs for adolescents, women, and individuals without health insurance. One conservative estimate, based on a survey of state alcohol and drug directors, is that only one adolescent in 13 is able to access treatment, in spite of evidence that every dollar spent in treatment for adolescents saves approximately $12 in later social costs.[13]

In addition to the lack of all forms of treatment for women, children, and youths involved in the child welfare system, there is a concern that many existing programs, developed to serve middle class clients, are less effective in addressing the needs of other racial, socioeconomic, or cultural groups. There is a critical need to respond by designing culturally responsive models for populations currently being underserved.

One of the key reasons why treatment approaches fail to achieve lasting results is the dearth of affordable, accessible, aftercare programs, especially for those returning to disadvantaged or heavily drug-involved communities. Public treatment centers often are able to finance only one month of outpatient aftercare in spite of the recognized importance of long-term support. Private clinics usually offer yearlong posttreatment programs, but they are far too costly for anyone without private insurance. There is a shortage of Alcoholics Anonymous (AA), Narcotics Anonymous (NA), or other ongoing peer support programs for nonwhite populations. These programs are often considered an essential adjunct to treatment to sustain recovery. However, of the 900 local chapters of NA, AA, or Cocaine Anonymous in Atlanta, Georgia, only 50 are in predominantly African American sections of town.[14] To be effective, aftercare programs must be located in all areas where individuals live and work, and must reflect the racial, cultural, and ethnic diversity of the population.

Juvenile and Family Courts

A judge now is able to dedicate an average of 10 minutes to each child's case. By 1995, judges will be allowed only five minutes to determine a child's fate.

—retired L.A. Judge Paul Boland

Because the courts make critical life decisions, a well-functioning court process is essential. In too many courts, decisions are delayed to an extent harmful to children; judges do not have time to conduct a thorough hearing; and court personnel and judges are not trained on issues relating to child welfare or the impact of substance abuse on children and families.

The courts, like the child welfare system, are in crisis—overwhelmed by rapidly increasing numbers of cases, and especially by increasing numbers of cases involving alcohol or drug abuse. There is general agreement among juvenile court judges that substance abuse problems have reached epidemic proportions for families involved with the child welfare system, and particularly among juvenile offenders. Courts are faced with overwhelming numbers of children from chemically involved families for whom they must make dependency adjudications, oversee ongoing case planning, and determine the appropriateness of permanency plans. For the young child, in particular, time is of the essence, but enormous backlogs and court delays often mean that decisions are not made in accordance with the developmental needs of the child for stability and consistency. The courts are also overwhelmed with chemically involved adolescents. One treatment official in Los Angeles reported to an American Bar Association Commission that 85 to 90% of the youths who come through the Los Angeles courts have an underlying drug problem.[15] Youth AOD abuse is a problem that the current court system has failed to adequately address, and without reform, may be unable to overcome.[16] Each juvenile court judge in Los Angeles is asked to make decisions affecting the lives of 350 juveniles a week.[17]

Little legislative attention has been given to the needs of the courts and the child welfare system in relation to these cases. At the same time, sufficient funds have not been appropriated to allow court orders to be implemented.

In response to this problem, the National Council of Juvenile and Family Court Judges has developed a decision-making protocol to help judges assess reasonable efforts and formulate treatment plans and orders in drug-related cases. Among the principles underlying the protocol: prenatal substance abuse may give rise to substantial harm or risk of harm to the child; to make good decisions, a court must have good risk data and an assessment of parental capacity for responsible child rearing; and prevention of substance abuse should be a goal of all systems.[18]

Despite its strengths, the protocol alone will not be sufficient to assure equity in decision making. Judicial training, the provision of trained counsel for children, and the use of court orders that clearly specify the expectations of all parties are essential. To assure judicial equity in decision making among diverse cultural and racial groups, there must also be greater understanding of the cultural and economic strengths and needs of each family.

The Health Care System

Financing Health Care

The alcohol and drug problem in this country is exacerbated by the real crisis in the lack of accessible, affordable health care and treatment. Thirty-two million Americans, including 8.3 million children under age 18, have no health insurance coverage.[19] Lack of insurance has a significant impact on health status. Pregnant women without insurance often do not receive prenatal care, increasing the risk of complications during labor and delivery and poor birth outcomes. Children who are uninsured typically fail to receive preventive care, and their medical needs are usually addressed only in emergency rooms and in times of crisis.

Existing services and programs have demonstrated some success, but the current approach functions mostly as a series of Band-Aids. For example: The WIC program supplies food and nutrition education to at-risk women and their children through the age of five. The program makes a significant difference in the health of the women and children it serves. A USDA study revealed that each dollar invested in the WIC program produces savings of between $1.77 and $3.13 in Medicaid in a baby's first two months of life. Only four million out of seven million eligible women and children, however, are currently served by WIC.[20]

Health care financing programs such as Medicaid and private insurance largely fail to provide sufficient coverage for preventive and specialty health care services, such as alcohol and drug abuse prevention, treatment and counseling; long-term treatment for serious or chronic illness; respite care; and mental health services.

Lack of access to health care is particularly grave in families where chemical dependency is also a problem. Chemical dependency carries with it many increased health risks that place the well-being of children and families in jeopardy. Nowhere is this need for access to preventive health care and treatment more evident than for families affected by AIDS or HIV, conditions closely associated with drug use. Approximately 32% of all adult and adolescent AIDS cases are related to intravenous drug use. Health care access is critical for the chemically dependent and HIV-exposed population.[21]

The health care system must also recognize and address the nonfinancial barriers to health care, including institutional practices, lack of transportation, limited availability of providers, cultural and language barriers, and poor coordination.

The Commission concurs with the recently released recommendations of the National Commission on Children regarding universal health care for pregnant women and children. Those recommendations call for joint efforts between government and employers to develop a universal system of health insurance coverage for pregnant women and for children through age 21, including care for problems associated with chemical dependency.

Coordination of Health Care and Child Welfare Services for Chemically Involved Women

Hospitals and public health care providers are increasingly being called upon to work with the child welfare system, especially in cases involving infants exposed prenatally to drugs. In some communities, hospitals and public health workers are becoming the gatekeepers for child welfare. They are asked to perform an initial investigation with a family, including home visits to determine if child welfare intervention is indicated. The use of a health care provider as the initial intervener has several advantages. First, contact by the health sector is less threatening and stigmatizing to the chemically involved parent, and therefore it is more likely to result in a positive outcome. Second, such intervention reduces the stress to the CPS system and allows limited CPS resources to be focused on other populations not connected with the medical community.

On the other hand, the child welfare system and the medical community have different, though equally valid goals. When confronted with chemical dependency, the health care system is primarily concerned with providing for the health needs of pregnant or postpartum women and their infants and children. Its goal is to assure that as many women as possible take advantage of pre- and postnatal services. For this reason, many medical professionals hesitate to make a referral to CPS even when they have reason to suspect that an infant discharged from the hospital with a chemically dependent mother is at risk of maltreatment. The child protective services system and its workers, on the other hand, are mandated to protect infants, children, and youths from abuse or neglect. They cannot fulfill that responsibility if they are not informed about situations that may place children at risk.

Some communities have attempted to support the goals of both systems through improved coordination and the pursuit of mutually agreed-upon policies and practices for chemically involved women and their children. When these community-wide, multidisciplinary, cross-system efforts have taken place, obvious benefits have resulted. These collaborations demonstrate that multiple systems can effectively provide interventions, if cross-training is available and mechanisms are in place to guarantee that the role of each agency is understood and supported.

Head Start/Early Education

The alcohol and drug treatment field, hospitals, the courts, and the child welfare system are not the only institutions experiencing the devastating impact of chemical dependency problems. As prenatally and postnatally drug-exposed children grow up, they enroll in child day care or Head Start programs, and then they enter school. The schools are largely unprepared and ill-equipped to accommodate their special needs.

The first large wave of drug-exposed children is now entering child day care, preschool, and Head Start programs. Head Start, a comprehensive child development program that serves over half a million low-income preschool children each year, is intended to serve both children and their families. The program attempts to help participants deal more effectively with their present environments and later responsibilities in school and community life. The emphasis is on the child's cognitive and language development and physical and mental health and on parental involvement. At least 10% of enrollment slots must be made available to children with disabilities. In addition, several programs exist within Head Start to serve HIV-positive children and children of substance abusers.

A number of Head Start programs report seeing increasing numbers of preschoolers who were prenatally exposed to drugs, and increasing numbers of substance-abusing parents. Both the physiological effects of drugs while the parent is "high" and the preoccupation with obtaining the next fix can limit the participation of actively drug-involved parents in programs designed to be a support. At the same time, the children themselves are clearly affected by chemical exposure. The programs report that although these youngsters usually score within the normal range in cognitive ability, they often display a range of developmental delays or atypical behavior patterns.

To address these issues, Head Start has awarded 41 Family Service Center Grants to demonstrate ways that Head Start programs can work with other community agencies and organizations on the problems of chemical abuse, illiteracy, and unemployment among Head Start families. The three-year projects will encourage families to participate in activities that:

- reduce and prevent the incidence of chemical involvement in Head Start families;
- improve the literacy of parents; and
- increase the employability of Head Start parents.

National Head Start staff are also in the process of developing curricula and training materials to help local teachers better address the needs of both children and parents. Specialized child development and education services are being emphasized in the belief that such services will enable many, if not all, drug-exposed children to compensate for drug-related deficits and reduce some of the risk factors associated with substance abuse.

Many substance-exposed children are already entering special education programs other than Head Start. Data indicate that the number of three-to-five-year-old children enrolled in preschool special education in Los Angeles and Miami has doubled since 1986, and New York City last year saw a 26% increase in its special education population, some of whom were exposed to drugs in utero and others who live in homes troubled by drug and alcohol abuse.[22] Services for school-age children have also been strained. Because of the variety of behaviors observed and the need to determine etiology, in-depth evaluations involving medical, social, psychological, and educational data are needed. The educational system, however, has not been prepared to provide such comprehensive services to the growing numbers of children needing them. At the same time, the educational system has been challenged to determine the appropriate educational placement for each child, to mobilize the services children need, and to educate teachers and staff to best meet these children's needs.

In July 1991, the Select Committee on Narcotics Abuse and Control held hearings on drug-exposed children and the schools. In his opening statement, Chairman Charles Rangel (D-NY) made the following observation: "Many veteran teachers say they feel alone. Although they know a problem exists, they often do not know how to identify, let alone counsel, drug-exposed children, and they rarely receive guidance or assistance."[23]

These problems are compounded by the fact that the

special-education system, like other human services, has evolved into a categorical program with specific eligibility criteria and funding designated for a targeted population. Many of the children served in special education also need services from the health, mental health, and child welfare systems. To ensure that children are well served, the systems must coordinate their efforts and focus their interventions on the needs of the child, often within the context of the family.

The importance of early educational intervention cannot be overemphasized. If sufficient resources for early intervention are not available, these children will have greater problems as they grow. The costs of providing appropriate learning experiences for these children, even when offered early, will be substantial. Those costs will only increase if early intervention is not made available.

Endnotes

1. Harner, I.C., "The Alcoholism Treatment Client and Domestic Violence," *Alcohol Health and Research Work* 12, 3, 1987: 150–160.

2. The Citizens Commission on AIDS for New York City and Northern New Jersey, "AIDS: Is There A Will to Meet the Challenge?" New York: Citizen's Commission,1991, 31.

3. National Association of State Alcohol and Drug Abuse Directors (NASADAD), "State Alcohol and Drug Abuse Profile (SADAP)," A Report for the National Institute on Drug Abuse and the National Institute on Alcohol Abuse and Alcoholism for FY90, Washington, DC: NASADAD, 1991. SADAP figures are based only on admissions to publicly funded programs.

4. National Commission on AIDS (NCA), "The Twin Epidemics of Substance Abuse and HIV," Washington, DC: NCA, July 1991, 5.

5. National Association of State Alcohol and Drug Abuse Directors (NASADAD), "Results of NASADAD Survey on Waiting Lists," Washington, DC: NASADAD, September 1989.

6. National Association of State Alcohol and Drug Abuse Directors (NASADAD), "Survey on Individuals Receiving Treatment and Additional Individuals Needing Treatment," Washington, DC: NASADAD, October 11, 1989.

7. Feig, Laura. "Drug-Exposed Infants and Children: Service Needs and Policy Questions," U.S. Department of Health and Human Services, Office of the Assistant Secretary for Planning and Evaluation, Unpublished report, August 1990.

8. National Association of State Alcohol and Drug Abuse Directors (NASADAD), *Treatment Works: A Review of 15 Years of Research Findings*, Washington, DC: NASADAD, 1990, 7.

9. U.S. Department of Health and Human Services (DHHS), National Institute on Drug Abuse, and the National Institute on Alcohol Abuse and Alcoholism, "Highlights from the 1989 National Drug and Alcoholism Treatment Unit Survey (NDATUS)," Washington, DC: DHHS, July 1990.

10. NDATUS 1990.

11. SADAP 1992.

12. Primm, Benjamin, Testimony before the National Commission on AIDS, Washington, DC, March 1990.

14. Gelb, A. "Black Communities Lack Aftercare for Addicts," *The Atlanta Journal and Constitution*, April 1, 1990, A-1.

15. American Bar Association (ABA), Policy Recommendations on Youth Alcohol and Drug Problems, Washington, DC: ABA, 1986.

16. ABA 1986.

17. Boland, P., "Perspectives of a Juvenile Court Judge," *The Future of Children* 1, 1 (Spring 1991): 101.

18. National Council of Juvenile and Family Court Judges, "Protocol for Making Responsible Efforts in Drug-Related Dependency Cases," Reno, NV: National Council, July 1991.

19. The National Commission on Children 1991, 137.

20. The National Commission on Children 1991, 1 and 151.

21. The National Commission on AIDS 1991, 1.

22. Schipper, W., Testimony before the U.S. House of Representatives Select Committee on Narcotics Abuse and Control, July 30, 1991.

23. Rangel, Charles B. (D-NY), Chairman, U.S. House of Representatives Select Committee on Narcotics Abuse and Control, Opening Statement at Hearing on Drug-Exposed Children and the Schools, July 30, 1991.

6

Improving the Delivery of Effective Services in the Community

The human service system faces special challenges as it shapes its response to chemical dependency issues. These challenges are manifested at the local community level by ineffective, unavailable, or uncoordinated services, which may also be unresponsive to the racial, cultural, and ethnic identity of chemically involved families. This chapter highlights the need for collaboration between child welfare agencies and the AOD field; the need for comprehensive, collaborative, community-based service delivery models; and the need for a non-deficit, culturally competent conceptual framework for services delivered to children and their chemically involved families.

Linking Child Welfare and the Substance Abuse Field

For too long, the child welfare community has not acknowledged its role in addressing and intervening into the chemical dependency issues that impact the children and families it serves. "We aren't in the alcohol and drug business" has been the common refrain. Workers are often oblivious to signs of alcohol or other drug abuse in their diligent efforts to protect children from other risks, which they are more comfortable assessing but which are often far less deadly. Likewise, the AOD field has traditionally addressed chemical dependency from the individual rather than the family or child perspective.

The myopia view of both the child welfare and the AOD treatment systems must be corrected. Child welfare agencies must forge partnerships with AOD prevention and treatment providers and the mental health and public health sectors to provide prevention and early intervention services to chemically dependent families. The AOD field must see the child welfare system as a potential ally in supporting and improving family functioning and in meeting the needs of the children in the family.

Isolated innovative programs currently in place demonstrate the power of partnership between the two systems. There are day treatment programs for mothers who abuse AOD that are linked with comprehensive child development or child day care centers. These efforts reinforce and support a mother's desire to get treatment, and they provide an opportunity for full assessment and intervention with the child. There are also residential child welfare centers linked to community-based alcohol and drug day treatment services for adolescents. Increasingly, family preservation workers in the child welfare system, unable to find appropriate AOD treatment programs in the community for many of the families they serve, are working with the substance abuse field to develop the competencies necessary to recognize and more effectively respond to chemical dependency issues. None of these efforts requires significant new expenditures. All of them require ongoing case planning, interagency agreement, effective communication, an attitude of cooperation between the agencies, and an ability to flexibly plan and deliver services at the local level.

The AOD prevention and treatment field and the child welfare system must also join forces to better protect the children of substance abusers. Research has consistently shown an association between alcohol and drug abuse and child maltreatment, neglect, and emotional abuse. The implications of this research for professionals are threefold: 1) all clients in either system with a chemical dependency history should be routinely and sensitively questioned regarding family violence; 2) all clients in either system in a violent relationship should be questioned regarding chemical use; and 3) all prevention and treatment interventions must take both family violence and chemical dependency into account.

Developing Comprehensive, Collaborative, Community-Based Continuum-of-Care Models

No single health or child welfare agency can meet the complex needs of today's chemically dependent families. Health and human service agencies working in partnership with alcohol and drug prevention and treatment providers must forge comprehensive, collaborative, community-based service delivery models. Varied agencies offering an array of child-centered, family-focused services must join together to promote the recovery of the chemically dependent individual; to address the needs of the other family members; and to strengthen and preserve the family whenever possible. The design and composition of services must recognize the changing needs of children and families at the various stages of the addiction process.

A major focus of a collaborative community-based effort between the child welfare and AOD fields must be the design and implementation of education and prevention strategies to target high-risk groups frequently found in the child welfare population. Child welfare agencies must work with AOD prevention specialists to develop the expertise necessary to educate their staff members, boards, and clients on the dangers of AOD abuse and to work for enhanced AOD prevention efforts at the community level. AOD prevention and treatment providers must work with child welfare professionals to ensure that prevention of alcohol and drug abuse is linked with community efforts to prevent child maltreatment.

In addition to education/prevention collaborative efforts, child welfare providers must be actively involved in advocacy efforts in behalf of chemically involved families by promoting the full array of needed AOD treatment services. Among the services that must be included in any community treatment model are:

Outpatient Alcohol and Drug Counseling Services

For individuals who do not require residential treatment in order to become sober and initiate the recovery process, accessible and affordable outpatient services are needed. Outpatient services must address the needs of the entire individual and not just the addiction. As previously stated, many chemically dependent women may need help in coping with violent or unstable relationships, resolving housing crises, obtaining job training, or healing from their own childhood scars of abuse or neglect. Many may require assistance in developing parenting skills.

The services should be linked in proximity and design with other age-appropriate counseling or child welfare services to address the needs of the children or adolescents in the family. Many children are at risk of chemical dependency due to their parents' AOD use; others need help in handling the environmental and emotional stress of being a COSA; and others will already be AOD-involved and will require services to break the cycle before they become dependent. In addition to counseling services for children, families may require extended child day care for young children or transportation assistance.

Residential Alcohol and Drug Treatment Programs
Designed Specifically for Women

Programs are needed for women who require residential treatment in order to gain sobriety. Successful residential programs include opportunities to improve the overall functioning of the chemically dependent woman as the most effective way to achieve and maintain sobriety. Programs must help women succeed not only in recovering from addiction, but also in building skills and abilities to help them function better in other areas of their lives—including their parenting and caregiving roles.

Whether or not the women have responsibility for their children while in treatment, the developmental needs of the children must also be addressed. If the program does not allow for children to remain in the setting 24 hours a day, regular, consistent, perhaps even daily contact will not only foster attachment, but also continue to motivate the mother to remain in treatment.

Some women may benefit most from programs that allow them to focus solely on their recovery without the day-to-day pressures of primary caregiving and parenting. If their children are in out-of-home care, the AOD treatment provider and child welfare agency have a responsibility to work together to promote reunification efforts by facilitating frequent visits in child-appropriate environments, providing ongoing case planning, and ensuring support following the mother's discharge from the program.

Sober Living Residences/Halfway Houses

For many chemically dependent individuals, the real challenge is remaining sober after leaving a safe, secure drug treatment program. Too often, all progress made can be erased when a newly recovering addict must return to a drug-infested, violent environment that serves as a powerful disincentive to recovery. Halfway houses should be designed to allow families to continue to rebuild their lives, practice new behaviors in a secure setting, and prepare for re-entry into society. For many, this also allows time to secure employment or safer permanent housing in order to make a new beginning.

Enhancing Collaborative Efforts

Regardless of the AOD program or setting, child welfare agencies should be included in the planning and delivery of services when children are at risk of maltreatment or neglect due to chemical dependency in the family. Child welfare providers must have access to services that protect the well-being of the child and promote the stability of the family. AOD services should be connected to the array of child welfare programs in the community, including in-home services, foster care, kinship care, residential care, and various youth services.

Interdisciplinary, interagency family/child treatment teams and protocols must be developed to identify and remove barriers to effective collaboration and communication at the local level. Interdisciplinary case management is necessary to assure that children and their families receive the appropriate mix of services. The case manager assigned to a family should work with the team to conduct a comprehensive assessment and implement a recovery plan for the entire family, centered around the needs of the child.

In a recent U.S. Department of Health and Human Services (DHHS) study of community-wide efforts in several cities to serve drug-exposed children and their families, it was found that most communities lack specific information on the nature and scope of their AOD problems, and as a result, are still in the early stages of addressing the specific service needs of these children and families. The study identified seven factors that shape a community's response:

- The existence of laws or administrative rules governing child abuse and neglect reporting;

- The state of the service delivery infrastructure before the drug epidemic;

- The focal point used to mobilize community resources, i.e., child abuse or maternal drug use;

- The severity of the drug problem relative to other social problems in the community;

- The range of professional disciplines involved in service delivery;

- The existence of planning, coordination, and training mechanisms; and

- The availability of diverse funding sources.[1]

Key obstacles to serving children and families on the local level include a lack of formal tracking systems or referral mechanisms for children, the rigidity of existing developmental program eligibility criteria, and gaps in the service capacity of existing programs.[2]

Comprehensive communitywide systems must have a secure, institutionalized, flexible funding base. The absence of long-term flexible funding impedes community efforts to meet the current and future needs of children of chemically dependent families. Many essential services may not be covered under existing funding mechanisms.[3] All of these obstacles must be eliminated if children and families are to be served effectively in their communities.

Creating a Non-Deficit, Culturally Relevant Conceptual Framework

Deficit models are as dangerous in addressing the needs of alcohol- or drug-exposed children, or their chemically dependent families, as they are in thinking about any group of children.[4] Too often deficits are used as an excuse for inaction or inappropriate action. Instead, child and family serving agencies must use a risk model which recognizes that fetal AOD exposure or a chemically involved family environment may compromise the child's developmental status, but appropriate interventions can significantly improve the child's potential for healthy growth and development and the family's potential for recovery.

Perceptions of risk must not blind the system or the decision makers to the strengths inherent in children and their families. Regardless of the intervention chosen, child welfare should encourage and support all caregivers to provide opportunities that can maximize the child's development. Training should empower and encourage caregivers to foster healthy attachments and feelings of self-worth.

All children and families are also entitled to services delivered in a culturally competent manner. This means that the child welfare and AOD fields must be aware of and respect the ethnic and cultural diversity of the families served and must be able to respond to the history, beliefs, values, and communication and behavior patterns that characterize the racial, ethnic, and cultural groups found in our society.

In working with African American families, for example, the child welfare system has realized great success when the service takes place in a context that recognizes the strengths of the African American culture and adopts a culturally relevant or non-deficit perspective on this culture.[5] In working with chemically involved families, professionals must draw upon racial/ethnic or cultural characteristics as resources to promote recovery and prevent relapse. In planning and delivery of prevention or treatment services, factors that serve as cultural/racial or ethnic barriers must be identified and eliminated.

Cultural sensitivity and competence are particularly important in decisions relating to out-of-home care. It is not a matter of debate that children of color are more likely to be removed from their homes and likely to be kept in care longer than Caucasian children. The child welfare system must evaluate all factors that may be contributing to this fact. When institutional bias against families of color is identified in CPS reporting procedures or investigations or in the provision of services to families, this bias must be eliminated.

Child and family service agencies are beginning to develop strategies to ensure that decisions and interventions are sensitive to the racial and cultural backgrounds of the children and families they serve. Agencies can become more culturally competent by recruiting staff to reflect the racial/ethnic diversity of the families served, developing training that focuses on culturally competent decision making, employing volunteer or professional outreach by individuals from the background and community of the children and families served, and aggressively recruiting and supporting caregivers of the same race and culture as the children placed in their care.

Endnotes

1. MACRO Systems, Inc., *Programs Serving Drug-Exposed Children and Their Families,* Vol. 1, Cross-site Findings and Policy Issues, Prepared under a contract to the Assistant Secretary for Planning and Evaluation, Washington, DC: U.S. Department of Health and Human Services, January 1991.

2. MACRO Systems 1991.

3. MACRO Systems 1991.

4. Weston, D., et al., "Drug-Exposed Babies: Research and Clinical Issues," *Zero to Three* 9, 5 (June 1989): 1–7.

5. Grey, S., and Nybell, L. "Issues in African American Family Preservation," *CHILD WELFARE* LXIX, 6 (November–December 1990): 513–523.

7

A Call to Action

Many things we need can wait, the child cannot. Now is the time his bones are being formed, his blood is being made, his mind is being developed. To him we cannot say tomorrow. His name is today.

—Gabriela Mistral
Chilean poet

National leadership is urgently needed in response to one of the gravest threats to our country's security. Drugs and alcohol are jeopardizing our children, destroying our families, and ravaging our communities. This nation is paying dearly in financial costs and human suffering.

If we are to save our children and preserve the integrity of our families we must have strong commitment, vision, and resources at the federal level which support, strengthen, and guide state and local efforts. Federal leadership must be matched at the state and community level by creativity and collaboration in planning and delivering services to children and families affected by alcohol and drugs. At all levels, we must have the willingness to invest in the professionals and agencies that serve these most vulnerable children and families.

Shifting the Focus of the War on Alcohol and Drugs

This Administration has spent $35 billion since 1986 trying to win the war on drugs. The 1992 National Drug Control Strategy and FY93 budget proposes to spend an additional $12.7 billion. This year, as in all previous years, there is an imbalance between supply reduction activities, such as national and international law enforcement and interdiction efforts, and demand reduction efforts, such as education, prevention, and treatment. In the current proposed budget, 28% of the funds— $3.5 billion—will go to state and local communities as the federal share of drug law enforcement, prevention, and treatment activities.[1] This amount falls far short of what is needed in local communities across the country.

The current strategy acknowledges that this country has a two-tiered drug problem. On one level, prevention efforts appear to be succeeding in reducing casual drug use in mainstream America. On the other level, hard-core, chronic use of drugs has remained constant or, in the case of cocaine, increased in recent years. The authors of the National Strategy conclude that chronic users are the most resistant to anti-drug messages and that progress will be slow and uneven in reversing the trends for this population. "Treatment and education stand little chance of succeeding if they must compete in a neighborhood where drug dealers flourish on every corner. That is why in communities hardest hit by the drug problem, inner-city and minority neighborhoods, law enforcement efforts are essential if demand reduction efforts are to succeed."[2]

The Administration proposes a number of categorical, targeted responses to address the problem of "hard core users" in inner cities and among minority populations. The proposed responses, however, fail in scope and tone to acknowledge the existing and potential strengths of families and community-based agencies in preventing alcohol or drug use and in promoting recovery. The strategy points to the violence and chaos found in drug-ravaged communities and focuses on law enforcement activities, with only minimal increases in prevention and treatment activities for families living in these communities. The plan does not address the urgent needs of children and families who are trying to survive and remain together amidst the chaos. The plan offers "more of the same." In fact, the 176-page strategy document contains little hope for vulnerable children and their families, and very few pages are devoted to issues directly related to child or family well-being. The plan targets users but fails to mobilize families or communities to reverse current trends.

For the first time, the National Strategy does address the problem of alcohol, the most deadly drug of abuse, but its focus is confined to underage, and therefore, illegal consumption. In the case of both alcohol and illicit drug use, the National Strategy bases recommendations on the premise that alcohol and drug problems result from "bad decisions by individuals with free wills."[3] As long as alcoholism and drug dependency are cast in those terms, responses will be misdirected. Alcoholism and drug dependency are serious public health problems that require prevention efforts and therapeutic interventions, not punitive policies and actions. Dependency is not a moral failing, and the problems related to dependency are not the result of willful misconduct. The Commission calls on the Office of National Drug Control Policy to redefine issues, redirect efforts, and balance law enforcement activities with the prevention, treatment, and aftercare services that are essential in order to address the needs of millions of chemically dependent individuals and their families.

Structural and Leadership Challenges at the Federal Level

The responsibility for programs affecting children and families is widely dispersed at the federal level. Mindful of this fragmentation, the Department of Health and Human Services (DHHS) recently underwent a major reorganization to place many of the programs it administers for children and families within one agency and provide greater coordination. The new structure incorporates child welfare and income maintenance activities within a new Administration for Children and Families (ACF). At present, however, coordination is only beginning to be established between ACF and the Alcohol, Drug Abuse and Mental Health Administration (ADAMHA) that administers alcohol and drug service programs for children, youths, and families and between those programs and the President's Office of National Drug Control Policy (ONDCP). To achieve the goals and objectives articulated by the Commission, the activities of ACF, ADAMHA, and ONDCP must be fully coordinated at the federal level.

The Office of National Drug Control Policy, the centerpiece of the Administration's drug policy efforts, and other federal agencies must pay more attention to the impact of the drug epidemic on children and families and on the systems that serve them. Greater emphasis needs to be given to these issues and more needs to be done in terms of the allocation of resources.

In part, fragmentation in the executive branch is a result of the fragmentation in the legislative branch. At least 15 Congressional committees have jurisdiction over various programs and issues related to children. Some committees authorize programs, at times with overlapping jurisdiction; some also raise revenues; and still others only appropriate funds. Similar parallel, duplicative, and confusing structures drive legislative efforts on alcohol and drugs. Given the existing structures, it is not difficult to understand why a coherent, comprehensive alcohol and drug legislation package to support children and families has never emerged.

Fragmentation and lack of coordination are also evident at the state and local levels. Communities often are constrained by categorical programming and financing. The confusing layers at the federal and state levels, designed to address specific needs in particular populations, make coordination at the local level more difficult for child welfare and alcohol and drug prevention and treatment providers to achieve. Communities must have more flexibility in designing and delivering programs to meet the needs of chemically involved families. Alcohol and drug problems do not occur in a vacuum, but service delivery is too often designed to ameliorate isolated problems rather than to address the complex and interrelated issues of the whole individual, much less the entire chemically involved family.

New Directions for the Child Welfare System

Reports of abuse and neglect have increased dramatically in many states due to parental alcohol or drug problems. Federal funding for child abuse prevention and services to strengthen and preserve families, for the provision of quality out-of-home care, and for reunification and aftercare services following placement have lagged far behind demonstrated needs.

Child welfare funds and services are clearly inadequate to address the serious problems confronting children and families today. Inadequate funding also serves to defeat service coordination for the children and families who come in contact with the child welfare system each year as a direct result of parental alcohol and drug problems. These children and their families should receive appropriate alcohol and other drug prevention or treatment services. In spite of inadequate funding, the child welfare field must recognize and respond to the devastating problems created by chemical dependency in families. Child welfare and other health and human service agencies must become actively involved in our nation's efforts to prevent alcohol and drug problems and to better address problems when prevention efforts fail. Advocacy efforts must be stepped up to assure that resources are realistically allocated for the numbers of children and families needing services, the current level of services, and the state of the child welfare system.

Action at all levels of government and within the child welfare field is critical to the development of alcohol and drug policies that address the comprehensive needs of high-need, low-resource children, youths, and families. This agenda must assure that chemically involved adolescents, children at risk of maltreatment, and families at risk of disruption because of chemical dependency are a priority. A comprehensive alcohol and drug and child welfare agenda must address service gaps, service barriers, and coordination issues that limit a community's ability to implement a full array of services, including education, prevention, early intervention, treatment, and aftercare. The combined alcohol and drug and child welfare agenda must address fragmentation through a comprehensive coordination strategy. Currently, the child welfare and AOD service systems operate independently from each other, using differing eligibility criteria, restrictive funding streams, and sometimes conflicting program requirements, creating a maze that severely limits access.

The Commission challenges the priorities of current national and state efforts and the policies and practices of many child and family agencies. As an alternative to the current policies and practices, the Commission calls for commitment and leadership at all levels of government and within the child welfare and related health and human service systems to adopt child-centered, family-focused alcohol and drug policies, programs, and practices, and to improve our ability to serve vulnerable children and families affected by alcohol and drugs.

A Twelve-Step National Policy Agenda

The Commission calls on the federal government—the President, the Congress, and the U.S. Department of Health and Human Services (DHHS)—and state legislatures and governors to make children and families a priority in their policies to combat the effects of alcohol and drugs by taking the following 12 steps:

1.   Place children and families at the forefront of our nation's alcohol and drug strategy by targeting additional funds to alcohol and drug education, prevention, treatment, and aftercare.

- The Commission calls for a National Advisory Board consisting of federal, state, and local child welfare experts, alcohol and drug prevention/treatment specialists, and child advocates, and public health, mental health, and education professionals to assist the President and the Office of National Drug Control Policy in developing strategies to benefit children and their families and in achieving a better balance between supply reduction and demand reduction activities.

- The Commission calls for a White House conference on children and adolescents in 1993 with a major focus on children and families affected by alcohol and drugs, and a review and evaluation of achievements in alcohol and drug education, prevention, treatment, and aftercare resulting from the shifting and refocusing of resources.

2. Create a policy framework for a comprehensive national alcohol and drug legislative agenda that addresses the needs of vulnerable children and their families.

- The Commission calls on the leadership of Congress to review existing legislation and programs that relate to alcohol and drug prevention and treatment and those that relate to the welfare of children and families in order to comprehensively address the needs of vulnerable, chemically involved children and families.

- The Commission calls on the leadership of Congress to facilitate greater coordination and collaboration across the authorizing and appropriating committees with jurisdiction over alcohol and drug and child welfare policies and programs in order to assure the development and implementation of comprehensive child-centered alcohol and drug legislation.

3. Provide all children, adolescents, and families with access to appropriate health care services for alcohol- or drug-related problems.

- The Commission calls for reform of the U.S. health care system to provide universal access to preventive, primary, and pediatric health care services, which include alcohol and drug prevention and treatment services as mandated benefits for all children, adolescents, and families. The health care system must recognize and address the nonfinancial barriers to health care, including institutional practices, transportation, limited availability of providers, cultural and language barriers, and poor coordination.

- Pending broader health care reform, the Commission calls for the expansion of Medicaid eligibility to require all states to cover pregnant and parenting women with incomes up to 185% of the federal poverty line, and to expand Medicaid eligibility to all infants, children, and adolescents who are placed in out-of-home care.

- Pending broader health care reform, the Commission calls for the expansion of Medicaid to include an appropriate range of residential and nonresidential alcohol and drug prevention and treatment services for all Medicaid-eligible pregnant women, women with young children, women of childbearing age, and children and adolescents who require such services. In addition, Medicaid-covered services should incorporate appropriate services for infants and young children who accompany their parents in residential treatment programs.

4. Prevent child maltreatment in chemically involved families by expanding and fully implementing community-based, culturally responsive services and programs to strengthen and support families.

- The Commission calls for the full implementation of existing authorized family resource centers that are neighborhood based and flexibly funded, and provide, directly or through referral, such services as alcohol/ drug prevention, treatment, and aftercare; parent training and support groups; child care and child development services; employment assistance; supportive housing; and recreational programs for adolescents.

- The Commission calls for an increase in the current 10% set-aside for women under the Alcohol, Drug Abuse and Mental Health Services (ADMS) Block Grant program to increase the availability of treatment services for pregnant and parenting women. Infants and young children are at particularly high risk of neglect or maltreatment if parents cannot get treatment for alcohol or drug problems, and treatment resources for women are inadequate to meet the need. The total appropriation for the ADMS Block Grant should be increased by an amount commensurate with the higher set-aside. The implementation of the set-aside should be subject to improved monitoring and data collection and should be enforced by DHHS.

- The Commission calls for explicit authorization and

funding for home visiting services for pregnant and postpartum women and their children. Home visiting services should be an integral component of all programs targeted to chemically involved families in the child welfare system.

- The Commission calls for increased support of interagency programs to conduct research demonstration projects on the prevention and treatment of child abuse and neglect resulting from chemical abuse/dependency.

5. Reduce the developmental risks to alcohol- and drug-exposed children through the expansion and enhancement of early intervention services.

- The Commission calls for federal incentives for the full implementation of Part H (established by P.L. 99-457) and Part B of the Individuals with Disabilities Education Act, P.L. 94-142. In order to ensure that every drug-exposed child in need of special developmental services, learning experiences, and/or structured learning environments receives such services, alcohol- or drug-exposed children should be included in the category of children who are at risk and eligible for early intervention services. Currently, states have the option to cover "at risk" children in the Part H program, but most states have not done so. Of those that have, the majority do not extend coverage to alcohol- or drug-exposed children. Congress should maximize incentives for the states currently in fiscal crisis to move forward with full implementation of the Part H program. Children who are eligible for Part H services (ages birth–3) should automatically become eligible for and receive services under Part B (ages 3–5). The Department of Education should ensure that the requirements of P.L. 94-142 are met for alcohol- and drug-exposed children who need special education services.

- The Commission calls for the enhancement of the Head Start program to increase the capacity and effectiveness of the services provided to alcohol- or drug-exposed children and families.

- The Commission calls for developmentally appropriate child day care services for children with special needs, including children exposed to alcohol or other drugs. The Department of Health and Human Services (DHHS) should permit, as part of the final regulations for the Child Care and Development Block Grant, differential rates for the provision of services to meet the special needs of each child.

6. Provide prenatally alcohol- or drug-exposed infants and young children in the child welfare system with the special services and consistent care they need for healthy development.

- The Commission calls on Congress to provide the full funding level of $30 million for the Abandoned Infants Assistance Act in FY93 with special attention given to collaboration between foster care agencies and health care providers (including public hospitals and children's hospitals).

- The Commission calls for extending eligibility for all Title IV-E services to all children entering foster care, particularly abandoned infants and children at risk of abandonment due to parental chemical dependency or prenatal AOD exposure.

- The Commission calls for comprehensive health examinations and treatment services for all children in the child welfare system, either through Early and Periodic Screening, Diagnosis and Treatment (EPSDT) under Medicaid or through another program that parallels the assessment and treatment requirements of EPSDT. Assessments should include screening and treatment for physical, mental health, and developmental needs associated with pre- or postnatal alcohol or drug exposure. The EPSDT program serves only one-fifth of the children living in poverty, despite the fact that EPSDT improves general health status and prevents serious disorders.

7. Improve and expand the delivery of alcohol and drug prevention and treatment services to chemically involved adolescents, especially those in the child welfare system.

- The Commission calls for discretionary grants through DHHS to fund state and local collaboration between the child welfare and alcohol/drug treatment fields. Joint projects should be initiated to deliver treatment and aftercare support services to adolescents in foster care and to homeless, runaway, and throwaway youths.

- The Commission calls for the extension of Title IV-E eligibility for foster care and adoption assistance through age 21, especially for adolescents with a history of alcohol or drug problems. These adolescents need transitional services and supports to prevent relapse as they move toward independence.

- The Commission calls for the extension of the Independent Living Program under Title IV-E to cover all adolescents in care through age 21. At present, extension to age 21 is at the option of the states. Eligibility should be mandatory for adolescents with a history of chemical dependency.

- The Commission calls on Congress to appropriate $20 million, the full authorization to provide services in the Drug Abuse Prevention Program for Runaway and Homeless Youth.

- The Commission calls on Congress to provide start-up funding for the Young Americans Act by appropriating $30 million for the program in FY93. In addition, $30 million should be provided for the Family Resource Act, bringing the total appropriations for coordinating social services delivery at the state and local level to $60 million. Once again, interagency collaboration is crucial to effective service delivery for this isolated and vulnerable population of children and families.

- The Commission calls on Congress to provide full funding for the Office of Juvenile Justice and Delinquency Prevention (OJJDP), the sole agency responsible for providing national leadership in juvenile justice programs. Programs related to community prevention efforts for juvenile drug trafficking and gang activity must be expanded.

- The Commission calls for full funding of the High Risk Youth Program administered by the Office of Substance Abuse Prevention, with a special emphasis on the creation of training and employment opportunities for high-risk youths.

8. Enhance and expand services for pregnant and parenting women and families at the state and local level by identifying and fully utilizing existing funds available under various federal programs.

- The Commission calls on governors and state legislatures to oppose nontherapeutic actions toward or criminal prosecution of pregnant women solely on the basis of chemical use or dependency.

- The Commission calls on states to review state policies/ legislation and the availability and accessibility of age-, culture-, and gender-appropriate alcohol/drug prevention, treatment, and aftercare programs for pregnant women and women with children, especially those in the child welfare system. Governors and state legislators should make family-oriented alcohol or drug treatment a priority, especially for families at risk of disruption. States, at a minimum, should comply with the women's set-aside in the ADMS Block Grant program, and fully utilize existing funds available under various federal programs, including supportive housing services, to maximize the availability of services to children and families.

- The Commission calls on Congress to enact legislation to appropriate $10 million for grants to the network of Title X clinics for outreach, counseling, voluntary family planning, and HIV-prevention services for women who are HIV positive or at risk for HIV infection.

- The Commission calls for statewide coordination of the activities of each department or agency that serves children and families, including social services, AOD treatment, mental health, education, housing, health care financing, and public health and income support, to assure that the complex needs of chemically involved families are addressed. Services called for in child welfare case planning and judicial reviews must be made available to children and theirr families.

- The Commission calls on state governments to identify and eliminate local barriers to integrating funding streams for alcohol and other drug prevention and treatment.

9. Increase funding for alcohol and drug training and cross-system skill building so that child and family service providers and direct caregivers can more effectively prevent and respond to alcohol or drug abuse in children and families.

- The Commission calls on state and local governments to assure adequate resources for cross-training among child welfare providers, the substance abuse field, and other agencies and professionals who serve chemically involved families.

- The Commission calls on state and local governments to facilitate participation of family foster parents or kinship care providers in AOD training by allowing child welfare agencies to be reimbursed for transportation, child care, and other related expenses.

- The Commission calls on the federal government to require states to set aside a designated percentage of child welfare Title IV-E training funds, matched at an enhanced rate, to develop and deliver basic alcohol and drug abuse prevention and treatment training for all child welfare professionals, foster parents, and other direct caregivers responsible for providing assessments, services, or direct care to children, youths, and families in the child welfare system. Basic training should enhance knowledge related to alcohol and drugs, the addiction process, and the impact of chemical dependency on family functioning. Staff members and caregivers who are responsible for direct service to chemically involved families should have additional training to improve their skills in assessing dependency and effectively serving chemically involved families.

10. Support child and family service agencies and caregivers in identifying and responding to alcohol and drug problems in the children and families they serve.

- The Commission calls on the federal government to require states to make assurances, as a state plan requirement for Title IV-B and Title IV-E, that every child or youth placed in care and every family served is questioned about alcohol or drug use at the time of intake and, when indicated, each child or family receives a full AOD assessment.

- The Commission calls for federal funding under Title IV-B or IV-E or other existing programs to assure that local and state providers have the resources to comply with a mandate to inquire about and assess AOD problems, and to secure appropriate AOD services based on the needs assessment.

- The Commission calls for a national minimum foster care board rate that is indexed to the cost of living and the age and special needs of infants, children, and youths in care, for reimbursement of family foster parents and kinship care providers. "Special needs" should include the needs of alcohol- or drug-exposed infants who require special care and attention, children of chemically involved parents, and adolescents who are alcohol or drug involved.

- The Commission calls for federal reimbursement for expanded respite care services for caregivers of infants and children with special needs, especially for alcohol- or drug-exposed babies who may require special care and attention.

- The Commission calls for federal reimbursement under Title IV-E for the full costs associated with recruiting, training, and supporting foster parents or kinship caregivers who are prepared to meet the needs of special-needs children, including alcohol- or drug-exposed infants and chemically involved children and youths.

11. Improve decision making by the courts and the legal system through training and supportive services that ensure the legal system's understanding of child welfare laws and alcohol and drug issues and sensitivity to the needs of children and chemically involved families.

- The Commission calls for financial assistance to state courts to provide AOD training for judges and court personnel to enhance their decision making regarding children and families in the child welfare system who are alcohol or drug involved.

- The Commission calls on judicial and family court judges to become fully aware of the availability of various types of treatment services in the community and to assure that all court-mandated services are available and accessible to children or families.

- The Commission calls for a review of state implementation of the Child Abuse Prevention and Treatment Act, which requires that guardians ad litem be appointed for abused or neglected children. DHHS should clarify and enforce this requirement and provide support to states to ensure compliance.

- The Commission calls on state governments to review current laws governing the grounds and time frames for termination of parental rights, to assure that artificial time frames do not serve as barriers to individualized decision making.

- The Commission calls for a review of judicial procedures by each state to remove barriers to an accelerated adoption process in the case of abandoned infants without options for reunification or in cases where efforts at reunification have proven unsuccessful.

12. Improve coordination at the federal level among the various programs for children and families and those that administer alcohol and drug programs, and with the Office of National Drug Control Policy.

- The Commission calls on DHHS to develop mechanisms for improving the collection and exchange of information, training, and resources between alcohol and drug programs and the child welfare system.

- The Commission calls on DHHS to review existing administrative policies to ensure that program development and implementation in both ADAMHA and ACF are coordinated to best serve the needs of children and families in the child welfare system. Coordination is essential in identifying and eliminating service gaps, fragmentation, and duplication.

- The Commission calls on the Secretary of DHHS to prepare an annual report on total DHHS discretionary and entitlement funding for AOD-related efforts directed toward children, adolescents, and families served by the child welfare system. The report should describe programs, document funding for these combined programs, and describe DHHS efforts to coordinate programs.

Recommendations for Child Welfare and Related Systems

The Commission calls on the child welfare system, including state and local public agencies and voluntary child and family service providers, to join with other health and human service agencies in reviewing and revising policies, practices, and agency procedures to ensure that they are responsive to the unique challenges posed by chemically involved children and families.

Taken together, these Commission recommendations make it possible for the child welfare system and related health and human service agencies to contribute significantly to our nation's alcohol and drug prevention efforts, to more effectively respond to alcohol and drug problems experienced by the children and families served, and to prevent and respond to AOD problems in the staff, caregivers, and volunteers who provide the services.

Enhancing Services to Children and Families

The child welfare system has eight broad, often overlapping areas of responsibility. Within each of these areas, the Commission believes that child welfare policies and practices must address alcohol and drug issues.

1. The child welfare system must protect and promote the well-being of all children.

The Commission calls on child welfare agencies to become more effective in preventing alcohol and drug problems that jeopardize the well-being of all children by:

Joining Community Education/Prevention Efforts
> Agencies must remain current and knowledgeable about AOD issues among the clients they serve and within their local communities.

> Agencies must educate and inform children and families about the dangers associated with alcohol and drugs and attempt to prevent alcohol and drug problems.

> Agencies must coordinate prevention and AOD awareness activities with the community's overall prevention efforts.

Developing AOD Education Activities

Agencies must develop activities to educate board and staff members, caregivers, and the lay community on issues related to chemical dependency and the impact of AOD abuse on the well-being of children and families and on the child welfare system.

Agencies must designate staff with AOD expertise to develop and monitor agency AOD policies and activities. Agencies should regularly review and evaluate AOD policies and activities to reflect changing client and community needs.

Agencies must deliver age-appropriate, culturally relevant alcohol and drug awareness and education messages and activities to all children, adolescents, and families served.

Advocating for More Responsive Alcohol and Drug Public Policies

Agencies must recognize that advocacy and community collaborations are important aspects of child welfare agencies' efforts in behalf of children and families. Agencies must build on their potential to make a unique contribution to community responses to children and parents affected by AOD problems.

Agencies must promote to the community at large AOD policies and programs that reflect an understanding of the nature of addiction and the needs of chemically involved families, and advocate for comprehensive, community-based, culturally relevant, family-focused alcohol and drug education, prevention, and treatment services for all children, adolescents, and families.

Agencies must promote public policies that ensure access to treatment for all individuals in need. In the case of adolescents, agencies should assure that policies regarding parental consent do not serve as barriers to receiving treatment services.

2. The child welfare system must support families and prevent problems that may result in the neglect, abuse, exploitation, or delinquency of children.

The Commission calls on child welfare agencies to improve child protection and family support policies and practices by:

Providing Appropriate Services to Protect Children of Substance Abusers

Child welfare agencies must recognize that parental alcohol and drug dependency place children at risk of abuse and neglect.

Child welfare agencies must provide services to children living with chemically involved parents. Services must attempt to undo the effects of abuse and neglect, stabilize the family, improve parenting skills, and prevent maltreatment. Child abuse prevention efforts, parenting training, and appropriate AOD treatment services can reduce child maltreatment and allow families to remain together.

In addition, child welfare agencies should assess the need for support groups, counseling, housing assistance, accessible medical care, education, job training programs, and child day care. When needs are identified, child welfare agencies must coordinate and deliver services directly or through collaborative efforts.

Recognizing the Vulnerability of Children in the Child Welfare System

Child welfare agencies must recognize that children and youths in the child welfare system are at high risk of developing alcohol or drug problems.

Child welfare agencies must recognize and address AOD issues and integrate them into their programs and services in order to enhance the identification of AOD problems and the success of early intervention efforts with chemically involved families.

Child welfare agencies must include alcohol and drug abuse prevention and early intervention services among the services provided to all children and youths in out-of-home care.

Child welfare agencies must review existing services and programs to determine their capacity to serve chemically involved children, youths, and their families.

Providing Appropriate Services to Strengthen Chemically Involved Families

Child welfare agencies must recognize that alcohol and drug problems are amenable to prevention and remediation when appropriate services are provided.

Child welfare agencies should expand and enhance services to strengthen and support chemically dependent families to allow them, when in the child's best interests, to retain or regain custody of their children. In determining whether in-home family preservation or support services are appropriate, workers must assess:

- the impact of AOD use on parental functioning,

- the level of parents' commitment to care for their children,

- the level of attachment between the child and parent,

- the support and involvement of relatives and kin in making plans and caring for the child,

- the willingness of parents to address AOD problems,

• the availability and accessibility of appropriate community AOD resources,

• the availability of active case management to assure that parents and children receive the services needed from multiple agencies, and, most importantly, and

• the ability to assure the safety and well-being of children in the home while chemical dependency issues are being addressed.

Building on the Community's Prevention/Early Intervention Services
Child welfare agencies must join with other community agencies and AOD providers to plan and implement effective prevention and early intervention services.

An effective prevention and early intervention program for chemically dependent families must be: child-centered and family-focused; based in communities where children and families work, live, and play; developmentally and age appropriate; culturally sensitive to reflect the diverse needs of families in the community; responsive to the transitions that children and families experience in their AOD use and recovery patterns; and staffed by competent individuals who have a solid knowledge of addictions and their impact on families.

Supporting Parents in Addressing AOD Issues
Child welfare agencies must encourage and motivate chemically involved parents to attend appropriate AOD treatment. Child welfare agencies must assist parents to participate in treatment through the provision of various services, which might include:

• referral to an AOD outpatient program,

- transportation to the AOD program,
- child day care,
- respite care,
- the provision of in-home services, and
- parenting skills programs.

3. The child welfare system must protect children and promote family stability by identifying and assessing family problems and providing the support necessary to resolve those problems.

The Commission calls on child welfare agencies to improve identification and assessment policies and practices by:

Assessing AOD Issues in All Children and Families Served
The agency must identify and assess alcohol and other drug (AOD) use/abuse in all children, youths, and families served. The agency must provide AOD training to staff members who are responsible for assessing family strengths and needs.

Agencies must include an alcohol and drug history as part of the intake process for all children and families served. When chemical use is present in a family, assessments made throughout the casework process must attempt to evaluate the impact of the chemical use by any family member on the safety and security of the children. If the initial intake indicates that a child or adolescent is using alcohol or drugs, a more comprehensive AOD assessment is indicated. All children and adolescents must be provided with appropriate services based on the initial intake and/or comprehensive assessment. The agency must refer and/or treat children, adolescents, and families with identified alcohol or drug problems.

Assessing Risk to the Child Posed by Parental AOD Involvement

Agencies must develop and/or improve child protective service assessments for children of chemically involved parents by thoroughly assessing the degree of parental impairment caused by AOD use and the related risks to the child. Assessments must be made on a case-by-case basis, but each must include a full evaluation of the nature, history, and impact of parental AOD use and its effect on family functioning within the context of overall family strengths and needs. All assessments must be conducted in a culturally competent manner by professionals who understand and value cultural diversity. Cultural or ethnic factors that can prevent alcohol or drug problems or promote recovery must be recognized and supported in all child welfare assessments and services.

Agencies must increase the knowledge and skills of all child welfare professionals who conduct risk assessments or provide services to families by providing basic training on alcohol and drug issues, the addiction process, and the impact on family functioning. Training is essential to assure that assessments are accurate, risks to the child are understood, and responses to chemically involved families are appropriate.

Appropriately Using Toxicology Screens in Risk Assessments and in Service Delivery

The agency, if it chooses to use toxicology screens as part of an overall therapeutic service plan, must develop an explicit policy regarding the use of such tests. Toxicology screens must never be used as the sole basis for separating a child from a family, but rather as a cue to assess the current service plan and intensify or modify services.

Child welfare agencies should regard a parent's positive toxicology screen as one factor in assessing the risk to the child, but should not use the screen as the sole factor. A positive toxicology or other evidence of parental AOD use, such as a self-report, should establish the need for a further, more comprehensive assessment of the family's strengths and needs and potential risk to the child. The assessment should place the toxicology screen results in context by fully evaluating the parents' AOD involvement, the level of attachment and commitment to parenting, the environmental risks, the parent's willingness to participate in treatment, and the family's overall level of functioning. This assessment is best accomplished by a qualified health or social service professional with special training in chemical dependency and family systems.

Using Toxicology Screens to Identify Chemically Involved
Pregnant Women or AOD-Exposed Infants

The agency has a responsibility to oppose efforts to criminalize the use of alcohol or other drugs during pregnancy. Chemical dependency is a serious public health problem and is best treated in the medical/ health arena. Referrals to child welfare agencies should not result in automatic referral to the law enforcement or criminal justice system. Such cross-referrals may deter chemically involved parents from seeking treatment.

Before or after childbirth, a parent's positive toxicology screen should be a basis for concern and should trigger a full assessment of the parent's AOD use and ability to protect and nurture the child(ren). If the further assessment establishes a basis for the suspicion of abuse or neglect, a report to child protective services, consistent with state child abuse reporting statutes, should be made. A parent's positive toxicology screen should not be the sole basis for a mandatory report to the child welfare authorities.

In instances where a child protective service referral is not indicated, but there is reason to believe, on the basis of the newborn's clinical presentation, that the child may be at medical or developmental risk and in need of follow-up services, referral must be made to a public health agency or other appropriate community resource.

When a newborn tests positive on a drug toxicology screen and/or there is other clinical evidence, following birth, of prenatal AOD exposure, a public health and child welfare collaborative investigation and assessment should be conducted to establish the health status of the infant; to determine any unique medical, social, or developmental needs resulting from the prenatal exposure; and to evaluate the family's ability to protect the infant and meet its needs. To be effective, a collaborative public health/child welfare investigation and assessment must be supported by cross-training and formal or informal interagency agreements specifying the respective roles and responsibilities of the various agencies.

Redesigning the Delivery of Support Services to Chemically Involved Families

The agency must encourage and support chemically involved families to care for their children and begin the recovery process.

Child welfare agencies must reevaluate the time frames for delivering family preservation services to assure that the long-term nature of chemical dependency is accounted for. If family preservation services are to end after a brief period, agencies must, prior to termination of services, link the family with ongoing, long-term resources in the community to continue the recovery process.

Child welfare agencies must plan for relapse and build in relapse prevention as a critical component of the service plan for strengthening and supporting families. Parents should be involved in planning for the safety of their children prior to relapse. Parents should be held accountable for failing to comply with the contingency plans and not for the relapse alone. Child welfare agencies should base evaluations of the success of services to preserve chemically involved families on their ability to promote the health and well-being of the children within the family, on the improvement in their parenting behaviors, on a reduction in problems related to chemical use/abuse, and on a decrease in other factors that place children at risk. Simply preventing out-of-home placement is not sufficient for chemically involved families.

Identifying Alternate Primary Caregivers

Child welfare agencies must assure that a child's health and developmental needs are being met while the child's parents are addressing AOD issues. In many cases where parents are heavily alcohol or drug involved, agencies must assure that an alternate primary caregiver in the family or kinship network is identified and supported while in-home services to preserve the family are delivered.

Working More Effectively with Juvenile and Family Courts

Child welfare agencies must work more effectively with juvenile and family courts to assure that children who are at risk of abuse or neglect due to the parents' chemical dependency are visible in the community. Mandatory AOD treatment should only be used when voluntary efforts to engage the parent have failed and/ or when the assurance of compliance is necessary to protect the child. If necessary to assure the safety of the child, agencies should work with the courts to mandate that families comply with prescribed service plans, which might include appointments for the child's medical or developmental care or for the parent's AOD treatment. Court orders to attend AOD treatment must be specific and realistic, with mandated case management and mandated documentation (weekly) between courts and AOD programs to assure compliance with specific court orders.

Appropriate, accessible AOD treatment must be made available to parents who voluntarily seek treatment or are under court order to attend. Families must be clearly informed that failure to comply with court-ordered services and prescribed service plans to protect the child and preserve the family could result in termination of support services and the initiation of proceedings to place the child outside of the home. Child welfare agencies must carefully monitor parental compliance with the service plan and/or court orders.

Children and youths in out-of-home care are entitled to court proceedings that are timely and skillfully handled, with the final decision based on the best interests and developmental needs of the child. When chemically involved parents are participating in treatment, decision making regarding the child should incorporate information from AOD treatment providers. Periodic reviews and assessments of parental progress in AOD treatment should be implemented and should be made available to the courts as one factor to consider in planning for the child.

Juvenile and family courts must improve decision making in regard to chemically dependent families by:

- Influencing the development of family law courses to reflect child welfare issues, child welfare law, and the legal, social, and psychological impact of chemical dependency on families.

- Providing cross-training to child welfare professionals and court personnel regarding the legal determinations affecting the child. The courts should recognize that parental AOD abuse frequently contributes to child maltreatment. Existing child abuse and neglect laws should be used to facilitate the participation of families in AOD treatment.

- Providing a guardian ad litem for all children of substance abusers referred to the court to assure that timely and appropriate services are provided to the child and that appropriate AOD services are made available to the parent(s). Representation of the child's interests separate from the interests of the parent or the state is essential, particularly when the desires of the parent are in conflict with the best interests of the child, or in the cases of children who have no advocates, such as abandoned infants or children.

- Ensuring that decisions affecting custody, separation of the child from the home and placement in care, termination of parental rights, or reunification include the evaluation of the parent by appropriate treatment professionals whenever there is reason to suspect parental AOD problems that might impair parenting and place the child at risk of abuse or neglect. Courts should utilize procedures in which the parent is offered the option of parenting classes, AOD treatment, or participation in other services as a condition for retaining or regaining custody of the child.

- Supporting the full implementation and funding of court-appointed special advocates (CASAs) for all children and youths who enter the child welfare system. Training on AOD issues must be provided to CASA volunteers to enable them to effectively intervene in behalf of children and families affected by AOD use.

- Requiring AOD assessments to be made of all youth offenders.

- Assuring that juvenile offenders in need of AOD services be given access to such services while in the custody of legal authorities. Judicial intervention should be utilized to mandate appropriate treatment for young people in detention.

Working with AOD Treatment Providers

The agency should encourage and support the further development and evaluation of an array of residential and nonresidential alcohol and drug programs for pregnant women and parents, including programs which allow parents to retain physical custody of their children while in treatment.

Child welfare agencies must work with AOD treatment providers to assure that residential programs that allow parents to retain physical custody of their children are not only designed to address the needs of the AOD-involved parent but also carefully planned to serve the unique developmental and other needs of their children. Such programs should be linked with a range of case-managed and drug treatment services and coordinated with the child welfare system to assure the well-being of the child upon the parent's discharge.

4. The child welfare system must place children in appropriate out-of-home care when continuation in the home poses a threat to the well-being of the child, the family, or the community, or when treatment is best provided in an out-of-home care setting.

The Commission calls on child welfare agencies to improve placement decision making by:

Improving Assessments Related to Placement
The assessment as to when separation of a child from a chemically involved family is appropriate must be made on a case-by-case basis. When there is evidence of child endangerment, and counseling, AOD treatment services for the family, and other efforts to maintain the child in the home cannot assure the child's safety, steps must be taken to protect her or him through an appropriate out-of-home placement. Placements should take into account the child's racial, cultural, and ethnic heritage.

Child welfare agencies must support and assist parents who require residential AOD treatment in voluntarily finding ways to assure the safety and well-being of their children through alternate care arrangements in kinship care or family foster care in order to facilitate parental access to and participation in treatment.

Matching the Child's and Family's Needs with the Most Appropriate Setting

Children who must be separated from their families are entitled to receive the most appropriate, least restrictive out-of-home care possible, and if AOD problems contributed to their placement, they must be provided opportunities to address concerns related to their own or their families' AOD use/abuse.

Child welfare agencies must conduct a thorough assessment of the individual child's strengths and needs and attempt to place the child in the program and setting that best meets his or her needs. The child welfare system must examine the appropriateness of each out-of-home care option. Such examinations should occur on a case-by-case basis when placement decisions are made. The final placement choice must be determined by the child's physical, emotional, and developmental needs. Child welfare agencies must engage the family to the fullest extent possible in decision making regarding placement for the child.

Child welfare agencies must assure that any placement, whether in kinship care, family foster care, or group or residential care, provides the child with a sense of stability, provides consistent, predictable, loving relationships, and assures that a child's developmental and safety needs are met.

Child welfare agencies must assess AOD issues in the child or family and develop interagency agreements to ensure that children or adolescents placed in out-of-home care receive appropriate AOD services not provided directly by the agency.

Agencies must advocate for the full array of placement

options, including kinship care, family foster care, and a range of group and residential care choices, in order to assure that children are placed in the most appropriate setting possible.

5. The child welfare system must assure that quality services are appropriately provided to children and adolescents in out-of-home care.

The Commission calls on child welfare agencies to enhance services and programs for children and adolescents placed in out-of-home care who are affected by alcohol or drugs by:

Meeting Each Child's Developmental Needs
Agencies must assure that the unique, individual developmental needs of each child in kinship care, family foster care, residential care, or group care are assessed, and that services are designed to meet the developmental needs of children of all ages.

Child welfare agencies must engage in collaborative efforts to develop or adapt comprehensive, age-appropriate assessment tools for drug-exposed infants, children, and youths.

Child welfare agencies must develop and provide additional social work and support services targeted to specifically meet the medical, mental health, and developmental needs of infants, children, and adolescents who are affected by AOD.

Assuring Placement Stability
Agencies must recognize the critical attachment and developmental needs of all children. In the case of infants, especially AOD-exposed infants, agencies must recognize critical needs for stability and security. Agencies must recognize the developmental harm that may

occur when any child or youth is subjected to multiple out-of-home care placements. Agencies must recognize that children and youths who are placed in out-of-home care, irrespective of the reason for initial placement, are at high risk for developing alcohol or drug problems.

Child welfare agencies must recognize and support a child's need for attachment when reviewing the case plan for any child in care. Child welfare agencies and the courts must recognize the trauma caused by moving a child from one placement to another. No child should be moved from an appropriate, safe, and stable placement solely on the basis of fiscal or systemic considerations.

Child welfare agencies must ensure that placements are stable by carefully matching the child's needs with the appropriate out-of-home care option, and by adequately supporting kinship care and foster care providers.

Child welfare agencies must provide adequate reimbursement to all caregivers, and facilitate their access to the services children need, especially when caregivers are responsible for children with complex needs. Services should include respite care, transportation, and child day care services.

Child welfare agencies must develop and implement procedures so that they can respond to any crisis in the caregiver's home on a 24-hour basis.

Child welfare agencies must carefully consider how many infants or children who are HIV infected, prenatally AOD exposed, or medically fragile should be placed in the same family foster or kinship home. Child welfare agencies must work with kinship families and foster parents to assess together their strengths, abilities, and preferences in reaching decisions regarding the number of such children that can be appropriately cared for in a family foster or kinship care home.

Child welfare agencies responsible for providing case management services to children in out-of-home care must assure that the caseload is low enough to allow workers time to fulfill their responsibilities to the child and the caregiver. Adequate resources must be provided to ensure lower caseloads.

Assuring Visits between Children and Chemically Involved Parents
Child welfare agencies must support consistent, frequent visits between children placed in out-of-home care and their chemically involved parents, whenever possible and appropriate, in order to support existing attachments and connections with the biological family.

Child welfare agencies must utilize visits as an assessment tool. Visits should be used to assess the strengths and needs of parents in relation to their parenting roles, to determine the appropriate scope of reasonable efforts for reunification, and to document that reasonable efforts are being made toward reunification. Child welfare agencies must work to eliminate barriers to visiting, including distance, lack of transportation, lack of child care for other children, inadequate staff resources, or lack of interagency agreements.

Assuring the Provision of AOD Services for Children and Youths
Agencies have the responsibility to provide, directly or through referral, alcohol and other drug treatment or aftercare services to children and adolescents in out-of-home care as an integral component of service delivery.

Given the shortage of available, affordable, appropriate prevention and treatment programs for adolescents, child welfare agencies, including residential facilities, must reevaluate and adapt their programs or practices to assure that AOD issues are addressed. Children or adolescents with a chemical dependency problem must be given treatment services either directly by the child welfare agency or through interagency agreement with AOD providers. If the child welfare provider is unable to provide appropriate AOD services, referral mechanisms and funds must be developed to assure assessment, treatment, or aftercare services by AOD providers in the community.

Agencies must be sensitive to the special needs of AOD-involved youths, who need ongoing support for recovery while in foster care and after leaving foster care.

Addressing HIV/AIDS

An array of prevention and treatment services related to HIV and AIDS must be available to all children, youths, and families served by the child welfare system. HIV/AIDS prevention activities, voluntary testing for HIV, counseling, primary and specialized health care, case management, and coordination with community resources are essential.

Providing Support to Caregivers

Agencies must recognize that kinship care is an important option that should be considered for children who need to be separated from chemically involved parents. Agencies must assist kinship caregivers in addressing AOD issues related to the parent's chemical abuse/dependency.

Agencies must question kinship caregivers and family foster parents about AOD involvement as part of the initial screening and assessment process.

Child welfare agencies must recognize that AOD use/abuse can impair any caregiver's ability to provide consistent, quality care.

Agencies must provide AOD training to all caregivers as part of their preservice and in-service training to ensure that they understand alcohol and drug issues and the impact of AOD abuse on the family. All direct care staff in residential settings and all foster parents and kinship caregivers should also be trained to develop the skills necessary to recognize and appropriately respond to AOD problems in the children and families they serve.

Caregivers must be supported to effectively relate to chemically involved parents of children in care.

Child welfare agencies must support and train kinship providers to be able to assure the safety and well-being of the child while managing the relationship and contact with the chemically dependent parent. Child welfare policies and practices must be adapted to reflect the difference inherent in dealing with kinship caregivers.

Kinship care providers, who may opt for permanent guardianship, must be assured of ongoing, periodic services and supports to maintain child well-being and family stability.

Agencies must support caregivers in meeting the special needs of prenatally AOD-exposed infants and toddlers. All direct caregivers must be trained in the care and handling of infants with special needs related to AOD exposure or other medical conditions. The number of caregivers must be limited and the environment must be structured to meet the special needs of the child for attachment.

Agencies must support foster parents and kinship caregivers in providing attentive and nurturing care and in meeting the child's changing physical, developmental, and psychological needs. Agencies must provide ongoing consultation and appropriate levels of support, including respite care, transportation, and child day care.

Agencies must include foster parents and kinship caregivers as part of the team of service providers. They should become active participants in decision making related to the children in their care, and they should receive training and specialized services to help them assume this role.

6. The child welfare system must reunite families from which children have been separated by providing services and supports to address the problems that led to placement.

The Commission calls on child welfare agencies to address AOD issues in permanency planning by:

Improving Permanency Planning

Child welfare agencies must carefully assess the child's and family's readiness for reunification by examining the family's overall strengths and needs, the availability of services to support reunification, and the developmental and other needs of the child. Specifically, reunification decisions should take into account such factors as: past history of abandonment or inability to locate parents, prior parental history of child abuse, placement of other children in care, prior unsuccessful efforts at reunification, history of drug-exposed births, level of motivation to parent a child, and the nature of impairment posed by any continuing AOD use.

Child welfare agencies must carefully evaluate permanency planning options on a case-by-case basis when appropriate AOD treatment is not available for parents who have children in care. Decisions must take into account the developmental needs of the child, parental strengths and abilities, parental compliance with other aspects of the service plans, and any unique family circumstances that would help to support reunification.

Child welfare agencies must clearly define objectives and expectations for each course of action being considered in permanency planning. Contractual agreements with biological parents should specify the expectations that the agency and court have for the parent, the agency's role in supporting the parents' efforts toward reunification, and the time frames for decision making.

Biological parents, foster parents, or other caregivers must be involved in the decision-making process regarding permanency planning.

When working with chemically involved parents, there must be an ongoing evaluation of the parent's efforts to obtain, participate in, and benefit from alcohol or drug treatment.

Child welfare agencies must not make success or failure of the parent in AOD treatment the sole factor in reunification decision making. Decisions must also consider the parent's ability to resume caregiving and assure safety of the child.

The needs of chemically dependent parents must be addressed when child welfare agencies make reasonable efforts to reunify families. Chemically dependent parents must receive appropriate AOD treatment services, including residential treatment, prior to termination of parental rights.

Permanency Planning for Infants and Young Children
Child welfare agencies must carefully monitor the child's stay in care, while assuring that efforts are ongoing to remedy the conditions that led to placement and that reunification or another plan for permanency is proceeding in a time frame consistent with the child's needs and best interests. This is particularly critical for infants and young children who are placed in care. Every effort should be made to assure that developmental needs are met and to expedite reunification or another permanent plan within time frames that meet the child's needs.

Working with AOD Treatment Providers in Permanency Planning
Child welfare agencies must establish and maintain ongoing contact with AOD service providers who work with chemically dependent parents. AOD providers must keep child welfare agencies informed about treatment progress, episodes of relapse, and/or unplanned discharge. Child welfare agencies must utilize such information in planning with the parent for the child and in developing a plan to prevent and respond to relapse and enhance opportunities for reunification.

Child welfare agencies must work with AOD providers to clarify confidentiality requirements and to assure that the parent's treatment plan is consistent with the child's case plan.

Exploring Permanent Alternatives to Reunification

Reunification may not be possible or appropriate for some children or adolescents in care.

In some cases the child's best interests may require that he or she not be reunited with the biological family. The possibility that reunification cannot be achieved should be recognized and relinquishment counseling should be part of the process of terminating parental rights. Child welfare agencies should support staff members who provide reunification/relinquishment services to parents, in order to resolve conflicts that may arise.

When an alcohol- or drug-exposed infant or child is abandoned, agencies must make diligent and timely efforts to locate the child's parents. When such efforts fail, and the court declares a child abandoned, child welfare agencies should expedite efforts to terminate parental rights and facilitate an adoption or other plan intended to be permanent for the child, including the possibility of kinship care.

Agencies must place children for whom reunification is unlikely in appropriate out-of-home care settings. When a full assessment leads to the conclusion that reunification is unlikely, every effort should be made to place AOD-exposed infants or young children with foster parents who understand and accept the role of foster parent but are also pre-approved and prepared to adopt the child if he or she is freed for adoption. Initial placements should take into account the cultural, ethnic, and racial heritage of the child, and every effort should be made to place children with kin or foster parents who are of the same race and culture as the child.

When reunification is unlikely, child welfare agencies

must pursue other permanency options for infants or young children, such as kinship care, adoption, or legal guardianship, while continuing to evaluate the possibility of reunification.

If, because of the child's developmental needs or best interests, the options of reunification and termination of parental rights are to be considered simultaneously and not sequentially, biological parents must be told that both options are under consideration. They should be kept informed; given clear and consistent messages by the courts, caseworkers, and foster parents; and encouraged to become active participants in the decision making.

Child welfare agencies should utilize expedited case reviews when individual circumstances indicate that reunification is not possible.

Providing Post-Reunification Services

Child welfare agencies must recognize that recovery is a lifelong process. The uneven path to recovery must be taken into account in planning for chemically dependent individuals. Chemically involved individuals and families who are reunited will need variable levels of support to assure the success of the permanent plan.

Child welfare agencies and the courts must include relapse prevention plans as part of the permanency planning for chemically involved children, adolescents, or families. Agencies must develop contingency plans with the child and family to assure the health and safety of children during times of parental relapse.

Agencies must provide, or assure through referral, ongoing relapse prevention and family support services for an extended time (18 months) after a child has been reunited with a parent who is beginning the recovery process, in order to prevent relapse and maximize the success of reunification efforts.

Agencies must actively engage extended family, foster parents, kin, and community resources in supporting the recovery following reunification.

Post-reunification family services might include alcohol or drug aftercare services, extended case management, and shared family care arrangements that combine in-home and out-of-home care services, parenting training, child care, and respite care. Child welfare agencies must supplement crisis management with ongoing support to promote recovery and prevent relapse.

7. The child welfare system must place children in suitable adoptive homes or in other living arrangements intended to be permanent in cases where return to the biological family is not possible or appropriate.

The Commission calls on child welfare agencies to support adoption and improve adoption practices for children and adolescents affected by alcohol or drugs by:

Making Better Decisions Related to Termination of Parental Rights

Child welfare agencies and the courts must attempt to base termination of parental rights decisions on the unique factors in each individual case. Decisions must take into account the age, life history, and connection of the child to his/her biological family. Severing all familial ties may be harmful to children even when they are successfully placed in adoptive homes. Termination of parental rights may be particularly harmful when other options for permanency are not provided.

The child welfare system and the courts must determine which set of circumstances indicates that reunification efforts are unlikely to succeed and then weigh the benefits and costs to the child of terminating parental rights. Termination decisions should be focused on the child's needs in addition to parental capacity.

Decisions must balance the serious risks posed by parental chemical dependency, the potential benefits, anticipated outcomes and predictable time frames for alcohol or drug treatment, the developmental needs of children, and the long-term consequences of the various child welfare options for the child.

While child welfare providers must actively advocate for opportunities for chemically dependent parents to receive the services they need to pursue recovery and resume their parenting roles, they must also recognize that in some cases a lengthy pursuit of reunification may not be in the best interests of the child. In such cases, child welfare agencies must promote policies and resources to support permanent placements with kinship caregivers or adoptive families. If children are placed on a long-term basis with kinship caregivers, it may not be in their best interests to terminate parental rights. Placement with kin and continued contact with biological parents can be a viable permanency plan for some children.

Recruiting, Training, and Supporting Adoptive Families
Child welfare agencies must recognize that chemically exposed infants and chemically involved children are adoptable.

When adoption is the permanency option, child welfare agencies should place children with same-race, same-culture adoptive families. Child welfare agencies must recruit, train, and support appropriate same-race, same-culture adoptive families for children who cannot be reunited with their biological families, including alcohol- or drug-exposed infants, children with chemically involved biological parents, or chemically involved adolescents.

Child welfare agencies must inform adoptive families if there is evidence that a child was prenatally alcohol or drug exposed. Disclosure demonstrates respect for the adoptive parents and ensures that children receive full and periodic assessments and, if needed, services to address potential developmental problems.

Parents who adopt children with special needs must receive postlegal adoption services. Child welfare agencies must recognize that postadoption services are sound child welfare practice in general, and are particularly necessary in cases of alcohol- or drug-exposed children. Subsidies for alcohol- or drug-exposed or HIV-infected children who may have special needs are essential for adoptive families.

Chemical dependency in the biological family is not necessarily a barrier to open adoption. Child welfare agencies must support ongoing contact after adoption between the child or adolescent and the biological family as a possible part of the permanent plan. Decisions regarding the degree of openness must be made on a case-by-case basis, considering the needs of all parties. The central factor must be the needs of the child.

Preparing Adolescents for Independence
Chemically involved adolescents leaving the child welfare system will need additional supports.

Child welfare agencies must assure transition into adult programs. Additional support will be necessary for many young people exiting foster care and preparing for adulthood. This is especially true when alcohol or drug use is a factor. Young adults who have a history of chemical involvement may require ongoing health care, referrals to substance abuse treatment and/or aftercare services, help with transitional living arrangements, and other supports.

Child welfare agencies must assess the chemically involved adolescent's individual needs and strengths to assure that services provided will enhance independent living skills and abilities. Activities to facilitate independent living should include services designed to prevent involvement with alcohol or drugs or to treat problems when they exist. Appropriate supports should be provided after discharge from the child welfare system and, if indicated, referrals should be made for ongoing services.

Child welfare agencies must refer adolescents with a history of AOD involvement to appropriate AOD aftercare services prior to discharge from the child welfare system in order to minimize the risk of relapse.

8. The child welfare system must take responsibility for identifying and ameliorating social forces that impinge on the welfare of children and families and intensify problems posed by chemical dependency, such as poverty, unemployment, inadequate housing, and lack of appropriate health care.

The Commission calls on child welfare agencies to address the total needs of chemically involved children and families by:

Recognizing Broader Issues
Child welfare agencies must recognize that alcohol-

and drug-involved families may be affected by broad social problems that extend beyond traditional child welfare issues.

Child welfare agencies must recognize that no single agency can adequately meet the complex needs of most chemically involved families, but every agency that serves children and families can assist in creating more responsive community-based systems of care.

Child welfare agencies must assess economic, social, and health needs when planning services for chemically involved children and families.

Child welfare agencies must create interagency community linkages to assure that multiple problems are addressed.

Increasing Advocacy Efforts

Child welfare agencies must advocate for the development of the full array of health and social services to assure that basic needs are met for all children and their families.

Child welfare agencies must advocate for increased funding for child welfare services and other services families need.

Recommendations for Enhancing Collaborative Efforts

Professionals working within child and family serving systems—child welfare, AOD prevention/treatment, juvenile justice, mental health, health care, and education—must review and improve current practices to enhance collaborative, community-based efforts in behalf of chemically involved children and families.

The Commission calls for child welfare and other child- and family-serving professionals to develop knowledge related to AOD issues, skills related to the provision of service, and strong collaborative ties with each other to address the needs of children, youths, and families who are AOD involved.

The Commission calls for:

1. Cross-System Education and Training

> Multidisciplinary, cross-system training relating to alcohol and other drug issues and the addictive process must be provided for child welfare agencies, the judicial system, and health providers on the local level in order to ensure that accurate assessments and appropriate responses are made to children or families who are chemically dependent.

> Child welfare agencies must be informed about the types of drug treatment and the range of services to which children, youths, and families should have access, and about the programs that exist in their community. Child welfare agencies must also work with the alcohol and drug treatment community to ensure that children and families served by child welfare have access to needed AOD services and that AOD services take into account the needs of all family members.

> Child welfare and other community agencies must develop multidisciplinary, cross- system team building and training to ensure that each system understands and accepts its role and responsibility.

> Child welfare agencies must develop policies that recognize AOD training as a priority and commit appropriate resources and time to facilitate this training. AOD training must be delivered by competent trainers with expertise in child welfare and chemical dependency, and should have clearly defined goals and measurable outcomes.

2. Increased Collaboration

> Child welfare agencies must support and facilitate intra- and interagency collaboration, including joint training and program development and resource sharing among the child welfare system, the AOD community, the courts, and other health and human service agencies.

> Collaborative efforts should ensure the coordination of all AOD services provided within the community.

> Collaborations should include case conferences among all agencies providing services for AOD-involved children, youths, and families.

> Child welfare agencies should establish both informal and formal interagency agreements with AOD providers to ensure appropriate AOD assessment, treatment, and aftercare services.

3. Case Planning/Management Teams

> Child welfare and AOD treatment providers and health care professionals must establish or participate in ongoing interagency, interdisciplinary teams for the care and case management of alcohol- or drug-involved infants, children, and families in the child welfare system.

> Agencies must establish or participate in teams that will assist with assessment of referrals, assessment of the risks posed to children by parental chemical dependency, case monitoring and evaluation, decision making regarding the appropriate course of action, and court reviews. The team should include, at a minimum, professionals in health care (such as public health

nurses or members of a hospital staff), chemical dependency professionals, and child welfare professionals. Representatives of other disciplines may be added as needed, including a government attorney as a resource for legal issues, a neonatologist, pediatrician, or addictionologist as a resource for medical issues, and a child psychologist for developmental issues.

The team should participate in establishing goals and clearly defining the roles and responsibilities of each member in monitoring the case plan for the child and family and in providing culturally competent services. The team must clarify how the issue of confidentiality will be handled.

Agencies participating in such teams are strongly encouraged to incorporate their mutually-agreed-upon terms of collaboration into written interagency agreements. By clarifying what the roles of intervenors are relative to each other and how each can assist the work of the other, written agreements can facilitate communication and service provision across disciplinary and agency lines, resulting in improved case coordination and services.

Agencies must ensure that all team members receive core training in the scope, dynamics, and treatment of chemical dependency; the effects of drug exposure on a child's health and development; resources to meet the unique needs that AOD-exposed children may evidence; and social work and legal aspects of child protection and placement. Such training is needed to establish a common frame of reference and an integrated knowledge base to support the team's case planning function.

4. Common AOD Screening and Assessment Protocols

> Child welfare agencies, health care providers, and AOD treatment providers must develop and implement appropriate AOD screening and assessment protocols to ensure early intervention.

> Child welfare and AOD treatment agencies and health care providers must routinely assess the use of alcohol and other drugs for all family members during the intake process, especially for women of childbearing years and children or youths at high risk.

> An appropriate assessment protocol will allow providers to tailor services to an individual's strengths and needs. In addition to addressing chemical dependency issues, assessments should identify needs in multiple areas, including parenting/caregiving roles. It is necessary to develop comprehensive assessments for tailoring services and evaluating outcomes. Assessments should take into account the needs of the individual user as well as the needs of other family members.

> Agencies and health care providers must develop standard protocols to routinely inform and educate both male and female adolescents, pregnant adolescents, and pregnant women about the dangers associated with AOD use during pregnancy, including the risk of HIV infection.

5. Comprehensive Risk Assessment Instruments

> The child welfare, AOD, and health fields must work together to develop a comprehensive family strengths and needs assessment instrument which evaluates parental competence in relation to AOD involvement.

> The fields of child welfare and AOD must work to-

gether to assure that the assessment instrument examines parental competence, the extent of parental impairment caused by AOD use or abuse, and the potential danger to the child.

Child welfare and AOD providers must work together to integrate child maltreatment risk assessment data into the routine intake procedure for admission to an AOD program. Providers, in the course of AOD treatment, must routinely assess the implications of drug-using behavior with reference to its impact on children and on parental capability.

Hospitals and other health care providers must routinely inquire about the use of alcohol and other drugs as part of the medical or psychosocial history obtained during intake for all women who present for prenatal care or delivery.

6. Improved Data Collection

Child welfare and related health and human service agencies must collect information on the prevalence of alcohol and other drug problems in the children and families served in order to assist decision makers and policymakers in understanding the true impact of AOD on vulnerable children, youths, and their families, and on the agencies that serve them.

The child welfare system must develop and routinely utilize standardized questions regarding AOD use/abuse in all intakes and investigations of child abuse or neglect.

Child welfare agencies must question all children, youths, and their families about AOD involvement at the time of initial intake. Information must be uniformly collected to allow for comparison and trend analysis. Practitioners must have adequate training to ensure that data are uniformly collected.

Child welfare agencies must encourage and support state and local efforts to establish reporting and tracking systems so that national data related to the impact of chemical dependency on children, youths, and their families can be collected.

Recommendations for Responding to Alcohol or Drugs in the Workplace

Voluntary and public child and family serving agencies also must review and/or revise their personnel procedures and policies to ensure that they are responsive to alcohol and drug issues. Chemical dependency is not confined to clients. Agencies must become more aware of and responsive to the needs of staff members, caregivers, and volunteers for alcohol and drug prevention and treatment services.

The Commission calls on child welfare agencies and other health and human service agencies to develop policies and procedures for recognizing and addressing AOD problems in staff members, caregivers, and volunteers. All policies and procedures should be regularly reviewed, in a manner consistent with local, state, and federal law, and should address the needs of individuals at all stages of the addiction process.

The Commission calls on agencies to:

- Review existing personnel policies to assess the extent to which they effectively prevent, identify, and address AOD issues of staff or other caregivers.

- Include an assessment of AOD involvement during the initial screening of individuals who are being employed as caregivers for infants, children, or adolescents.

- Conduct in-service training for all staff members and caregivers to promote self-assessment of AOD problems.

- Develop personnel policies that address AOD use by staff members or other caregivers, including written policies that clearly state the consequences of AOD use in the workplace or while responsible for children in care.

- Develop written policies regarding alcohol or drug testing. Staff members and caregivers must understand how the tests are to be used and who will be informed of the results. Toxicology tests, if utilized by the agency, must conform to all federal and state requirements. Alcohol or drug testing, if used, should be part of an overall agency prevention and intervention strategy.

- Develop written procedures for responding to staff members or caregivers who are suspected of being under the influence of alcohol or drugs.

- Review employee health benefits to determine the extent to which appropriate inpatient and outpatient services are covered. Agencies should work to develop employee assistance programs that cover alcohol and drug problems.

- Develop written drug-free workplace policies. These must cover the use of alcohol at agency-sponsored events.

- Review and/or develop policies regarding the acceptance of funds from the alcohol and tobacco industries.

The Commission calls on the Child Welfare League of America to review and revise existing CWLA standards as necessary, to reflect policies, practices, and agency procedures consistent with the Commission's recommendations for responding to AOD issues in children and families served and in staff members, caregivers, and volunteers.

The Commission further recommends that the Council on Accreditation of Services for Families and Children, Inc., the Joint Commission on Accreditation of Healthcare Organizations, and other national accrediting bodies review existing requirements to ensure that they reflect an understanding of, and an appropriate response to, problems of chemical dependency in children and families served and in staff members, caregivers, and/or volunteers.

Recommendations for the Research Community

Child welfare policymakers and providers have always been hampered in their efforts to serve children and families by insufficient scientific investigation into issues related to child welfare practice. They have had little data about the characteristics of the populations served, the problems encountered, and the effectiveness of different interventions with specific populations.

The Commission was charged with assessing the impact of alcohol and other drugs on child welfare policy and practice and with identifying related areas requiring further empirical research. Fairly substantial research has already been done on the impact of AOD on children and families in terms of epidemiology, the effects of AOD on child development, and the evaluation of various programs that either prevent or treat problems related to AOD in the general population. The research effort focusing on the impact of the widespread use of alcohol or drugs on the child welfare system's ability to deliver services, however, has been sporadic and fragmented.

Child welfare research as a whole has faced numerous challenges. It is often difficult to conceptualize and evaluate activity in the child welfare field because the issues involved are not easy to quantify. Even when issues can be quantified, child welfare organizations often have limited capabilities to collect, analyze, and report statistical data. At the same time, child welfare providers have traditionally invested more in service provision than in inquiry and evaluation. In recent years, child welfare resources have been particularly scarce, making expenditures on research rather than on services even more difficult to justify. Child welfare providers may also be wary of the possible negative consequences of evaluative research. Finally, funding specifically targeted to research has been limited. Government and private research funds have not been available to address complex questions through long-term service outcome studies. Ironically, because child welfare lacks a sufficient body of credible research on which to base future study, highly competitive research funding is more difficult to obtain. Because of these, and perhaps other factors, the child welfare field has historically based its policy and practice on research from other fields or on assumptions derived from clinical practice. This practice has resulted in faulty assumptions and an inability to demonstrate the effectiveness and quality of services, and is particularly problematic when alcohol and other drugs are involved. The lack of data on AOD issues in families must be addressed.

Movement toward encouraging state departments of social services to collect detailed and uniform statistics on the use or abuse of alcohol and drugs in the children and families they serve has been slow to develop. For example, the American Public Welfare Association, in a national survey of state CPS agencies, reported that out of substantiated reports of child abuse and neglect among eight states in FY88, 24.2% involved parental use of alcohol and other drugs, but no other states were able to provide such figures. There was only anecdotal evidence to suggest that increases in the actual numbers of children involved in substantiated reports of abuse and neglect in which parental use of AOD was a factor had resulted in increased numbers of foster care placements in the remaining states.[4]

CWLA, acting at the request of the Commission, conducted a survey of its member agencies on the impact of alcohol and other drugs on the delivery of child welfare services. All CWLA direct service member agencies (547 state, county, city, and voluntary not-for-profit agencies) were asked to participate. Two hundred and fifty-four responded, for a return rate of 46.4%. Complete data was collected from eleven state child welfare agencies: those of Alabama, Kentucky, Massachusetts, North Carolina, New Hampshire, New York, Rhode Island, South Carolina, Tennessee, Washington, and Wyoming. Out of 308,816 children served in FY90 by these public agencies, 114,412, or 37%, were affected by problems associated with alcohol or drugs, such as living with an AOD-abusing caregiver. Seven jurisdictions (Alabama, Massachusetts, New Hampshire, New York, Washington, Wyoming, and the Province of Ontario) reported that the child's own use of AOD was judged to be at least one of the presenting problems in 12% of the cases served by public agencies.

For the first time, the same data were collected from the voluntary, not-for-profit sector. Out of 111,927 children served by 129 private child welfare agencies throughout North America, 64,200, or 57.4%, were reported to be affected by problems associated with AOD, such as living with an AOD-abusing caregiver. Out of 89,106 children served in 100 child welfare agencies, the child's own use of AOD was judged to be at least one of the presenting problems in 21.2% of the cases. Higher percentages in the voluntary sector probably reflect greater efforts at detection and screening. Whereas only 15 out of 36 states, or 41.7%, reported routinely screening referrals for AOD problems, 125 out of 176, or 71% of the voluntary agencies reported that they routinely screen for AOD problems.

Respondents were asked if their agencies had ever served a "boarder baby," defined as an infant or young child abandoned at the hospital, frequently by parents with problems related to AOD. If the answer was yes, respondents were asked to report on the number of such infants served in the past 12 months. Because of a concern about duplication, e.g., voluntary, not-for-profit agencies counting the same infants or young children reported by their respective counties or states, no voluntary, not-for-profit data was used when data from a state was available. Respondents reported having served as many as 5,791 abandoned infants or young children in the past 12 months. Due to the lack of data from large states such as California, Florida, Illinois, Massachusetts, Pennsylvania, and Texas, this represents only a small percentage of the actual numbers.

Survey respondents were also asked to agree or disagree with a series of statements that described the potential impact of client AOD problems on their ability to provide services in seven program areas: family preservation, child protective services, adolescent pregnancy and parenting, family foster care, adoptive services, residential care, and child day care.

Respondents agreed that problems associated with AOD had increased, particularly in the past five years. When asked if the number of children either affected by AOD or using AOD was higher in the past year than in the previous year, 94 out of 200, or 47%, answered yes. When asked about increases in the past five years, 176 out of 200, or 88%, answered yes.

Types of AOD Use Identified by Respondents

When asked which substances were either "fairly commonly used" or "commonly used" among the children and families served by their agencies, respondents most frequently cited beer, wine, liquor, and marijuana. There were also high numbers for cocaine and crack cocaine. Regional differences appeared small.

Specific concerns were expressed about users of crack cocaine.

- 70% of the respondents said that crack cocaine is a serious problem among the children and families they serve.

- 88% said that users of crack cocaine are more difficult to work with than other drug users.

- 83% said that users of crack cocaine are more likely to be unpredictable or violent than are other drug users.

Respondents were then asked about their roles and responsibilities in treating problems related to AOD. Among the voluntary, not-for-profit agencies, 47 out of 175, or 26.9%, stated that their agencies should not take primary responsibility for treating problems related to AOD, but should identify problems and then refer children and families elsewhere. When asked if referral sources were accessible and affordable in their communities, 114 out of 174, or 65.5%, said yes. When asked if their agencies would provide more services related to AOD if funds were available for staff development and training, 126 out of 175, or 76.4%, answered yes. Currently, about half of all full-time direct service practitioners are reported to have received formal training related to AOD.

Impact of AOD on Service Delivery

Respondents were then asked to agree or disagree with a series of statements that described the potential impact of AOD on their organizations' abilities to provide services in seven program areas: child protective services, family preservation, foster care, adoptive services, residential care, adolescent pregnancy, and child day care. Despite the impressionistic nature of the data, consensus among the respondents was high.

Child Protective Services

Respondents reported that problems associated with AOD are increasingly a factor in child protective services (CPS). Problems both complicate and lengthen the investigative process.

- 93% reported that they are seeing more cases where problems related to AOD are a factor in the initial investigation, while 83% reported that problems related to AOD increase the time spent in investigation.

- Over 92% reported that AOD are increasingly a factor in reports of child physical abuse and child neglect, while 84% reported that problems related to AOD are increasingly a factor in child sexual abuse.

- 68% reported that families under investigation are routinely screened for problems related to AOD, while only 31% stated that risk assessment tools currently in use adequately assess the dangers posed by AOD.

- 88% stated that problems related to AOD are increasingly a factor in the dependency petitions they file.

- 64% reported that referrals of abandoned infants have increased because of problems related to AOD.

- 49% thought that CPS workers were reluctant to work with families with problems associated with AOD because of concern for their personal safety.

- 66% of the respondents stated that their agencies provided training in recognizing and dealing with problems related to AOD for their CPS workers.

Family Preservation Services

Respondents reported higher percentages of screening for AOD in the provision of family preservation services than in the other service categories, as well as higher percentages of worker training in the area of AOD. Nevertheless, AOD were perceived as contributing to the difficulties in providing services and in keeping families together.

- 91% reported that the number of families with problems associated with AOD served in family preservation programs was increasing while over 90% reported that maintaining children in their own home was easier when neither alcohol nor drugs was among the family's presenting problems.

- 73% of the respondents reported that families were routinely screened for problems with AOD while 78% reported that their agencies serve those families as opposed to referring them elsewhere.

- 95% thought that families with problems associated with AOD required longer service periods than other families, but only 36% thought that workers were reluctant to work with families with problems associated with AOD because of concern for their personal safety.

- 84% of the respondents stated that their agencies provided training in recognizing and dealing with problems related to AOD for their family preservation workers.

Foster Care

Results indicated severe strains in the foster care system resulting from the impact of AOD. Problems related to AOD contribute to the numbers of children who need out-of-home care, increase the length of time in out-of-home care, and complicate efforts at family reunification.

- 88% reported they are seeing more children entering foster care who were prenatally exposed to AOD.

- 94% reported they are seeing more children entering foster care whose parents abuse AOD.

- 53% reported they are seeing more children entering foster care who themselves abuse AOD.

- 87% reported that foster children prenatally exposed to AOD are more likely to experience multiple placements than children not exposed, while 91% reported that those same children are likely to stay in foster care longer than children not exposed.

- 87% reported that foster children whose parents abuse AOD are more likely to experience multiple placements than other children, while 96% reported that those same children are likely to stay in foster care longer.

- 99% reported that foster children who use AOD themselves are more likely to experience multiple placements, while 90% reported that those same children are likely to stay in foster care longer.

- 36% (52 out of 144) reported that, at least once in the past year, their agencies had not returned a foster child to a family because of dangerous drug activities in the families' neighborhoods.

- 69% reported an increase in the use of kinship care specifically for children exposed to AOD.

- 48% reported they are having difficulty recruiting foster parents for children prenatally exposed to AOD.

- 71% reported that foster parents who care for children prenatally exposed to AOD require more supervision than other foster parents.

Adoption Services

Respondents reported that it is more difficult to find adoptive resources for children exposed to AOD as opposed to children not exposed and that problems related to AOD increase the risk of disruption and increase the need for post-adoptive services.

- 93% of the respondents reported that they had placed children prenatally exposed to AOD in adoptive homes, but 84% reported that it is more difficult to find adoptive homes for those children as opposed to children not prenatally exposed to AOD.

- 98% reported that adoptive parents are informed of children's prenatal exposure to AOD, and 98% reported that adoptive parents are oriented to the potential short- and long-term consequences of prenatal exposure to AOD.

- 83% thought that children's exposure to AOD increased the risk of adoptive disruption. A full 98% thought that problems related to AOD increase the need for postadoptive services.

- 55% reported that adoptive parents receive special training in the care of children exposed to AOD.

- 52% reported that potential adoptive parents are routinely screened for problems related to AOD.

- 68% reported that their agencies provide training in recognizing and dealing with problems related to AOD for their adoption workers.

Residential Group Care

Respondents reported that problems related to AOD made caring for children in residential care more difficult and complicated efforts in returning children home or in finding foster care or adoptive resources.

- 90% of the respondents reported that they are seeing more children referred for service whose parents have problems with AOD, while 70% reported that increasingly children referred for service use AOD themselves.

- 56% said that all children referred for residential services are routinely screened for AOD, while 54% reported that children are referred elsewhere when problems related to the use of AOD are detected.

- 82% thought that children with problems related to AOD are more difficult to manage in residential care, 81% thought those same children require longer care than children without problems related to AOD, while 87% thought that those same children are more likely to experience multiple placements as opposed to children without problems related to AOD.

- 83% thought that it is more difficult to find foster care or adoptive resources for children with problems related to AOD.

- 78% reported that children in their care are asked about their use of AOD on a regular basis, while 56% reported that children in their care have their urine tested for AOD.

- 79% reported that their agencies provide training in recognizing and dealing with problems related to AOD for their residential child care staff.

Adolescent Pregnancy Services

Respondents reported that problems related to AOD are increasing among pregnant and parenting adolescents, while efforts at systematically identifying those problems, as well as resources to treat them, are limited.

- Over 81% of the respondents reported that the use of both alcohol and drugs was increasing among the female adolescents they serve.

- 55% stated that all pregnant adolescents referred to their agencies for service are routinely screened for AOD while 61% reported that pregnant adolescents are referred elsewhere for problems related to the use of AOD.

- 32% reported that their agencies provide medical case management services to pregnant adolescents with problems related to AOD.

- 35% reported that they are able to find appropriate residential services for pregnant adolescents with severe problems related to AOD.

- 64% reported that their agencies provide training in recognizing and dealing with problems related to AOD for their adolescent pregnancy workers.

Child Day Care Services

Respondents reported seeing more parents who use AOD, and thought that the number of children with developmental or behavioral problems related to AOD was increasing, while services designed to improve the developmental status of such children remained limited.

- 70% thought that more of their children's parents use AOD now than in years past.

- 56% reported that their agencies maintain specific policies and procedures about dismissing children to intoxicated parents.

- 91% thought that the number of children with developmental or behavioral problems related to prenatal AOD exposure was increasing, while 45% reported they provide special services designed to improve the developmental status of such children.

- 57% reported that their agencies provide staff training in recognizing and dealing with problems related to AOD.

On the basis of CWLA's preliminary analysis, the Commission concluded that the impact of AOD on the ability of the child welfare system to deliver services is profound and adversely affects the system by compounding problems, such as personnel shortages and inadequate resources, which existed before AOD was identified as a major social problem. Research is needed to further evaluate the impact of AOD and to explicate the systemic changes and stresses that they cause.[5]

The Commission calls on the research community to make chemically involved children and families in the child welfare system a priority in its research activities and to conduct evaluation research in field settings in order to maximize the integration of practice knowledge with the formulation of research questions. Research efforts should be sensitive to and address cultural, racial, and gender issues.

The Commission identified major knowledge gaps in four main areas. Research is needed to more accurately describe the numbers and characteristics of alcohol- or drug-involved children and families who enter the child welfare system; to evaluate the effectiveness of various child welfare interventions in preventing and responding to AOD issues that impact upon children and their families; to improve screening, assessment, and decision making for chemically involved children and families in the child welfare system; and to develop and evaluate model collaborative efforts between the child welfare field and the alcohol and other drug treatment community for vulnerable children, adolescents, and women in the child welfare system.

1.   Research should be conducted to more accurately describe the numbers and characteristics of alcohol- or drug-involved children and families who come to the attention of the child welfare system.

Much more needs to be known about the AOD-affected population groups served by the child welfare system.

Pregnant Adolescents and Women

While chemical use/abuse by women of childbearing age is recognized as a significant problem, the scope of the problem has not been determined. A number of longitudinal studies are currently underway by the Centers for Disease Control (CDC), the National Institute for Drug Abuse (NIDA), and the National Institute for Alcoholism and Alcohol Abuse (NIAAA), which should provide the most comprehensive data thus far. However, a mechanism is needed to collect this kind of information on an ongoing basis, especially for the populations that are served by child welfare.

There is also the need to know what chemicals or combinations of chemicals, in what amounts and at what points in the pregnancy, are most damaging to the fetus. Without such information, it is impossible to determine the specific interventions in prenatal care or drug treatment that are most effective in minimizing or eliminating risk of harm to the fetus.

Infants and Toddlers

An accurate, national survey has not been conducted to determine the demographics of AOD-exposed infants, the trends associated with exposure, or the short- or long-term medical or developmental problems associated with maternal drug use. Although NIDA and the National Institute of Child Health and Human Development have begun research in these areas, much more information is needed.

Children and Families

There is a critical need for accurate, complete, and relevant data about the children and families served by the child welfare system, including information regarding AOD use/abuse and the impact of chemical dependency on family functioning and parental capacity. Information could assist in accurately detecting trends and could help policymakers and decision makers in budget and program planning to meet emerging needs. With the inadequate data collection system now in place, it is impossible to definitely state how many children are in care or how many children are in care because of parental substance abuse.

Adolescents

Providers currently guess at the percentage of adolescents in the child welfare system who are AOD involved. There is no information on the role of AOD use in contributing to the actual reasons for the placement. There is no information as to whether adolescents in the child welfare system are using AOD in a way that is consistent with trends in the overall adolescent population. The unanswered questions about adolescents, in particular, reflect the lack of attention this group has historically received.

2. Research is needed to evaluate the effectiveness of child welfare interventions in preventing and responding to AOD issues that impact children, adolescents, and their families.

For each population group, there are many unanswered questions.

Pregnant Women

What types of AOD prevention efforts are most effective? What treatment efforts are most successful in stopping women from using alcohol and drugs? What social services most improve treatment outcomes? Are women who have been AOD abusers more amenable to treatment upon the birth of a child?

Infants and Toddlers

How do we explain the successes among this group: the infants born exposed to drugs who are not lagging by any developmental, physical, or emotional measures? What are some of the protective factors that account for "success"? Which interventions have been successful in reducing or reversing developmental risk? What combination of services has been most effective in improving developmental outcome?

Children and Families

How are chemical users or abusers different from chemically dependent parents in their parenting abilities? At what point does drug abuse impair parenting? How is parenting ability affected by the severity and frequency of drug use? Is the drug of choice the most significant predictor? What role do environmental factors play in the degree of risk for the child? What type of services are most effective in preventing future AOD involvement by children raised in a chemically dependent family?

Adolescents

How can we prevent initiation into AOD use in high-risk youths? What accounts for the fact that the majority of youths in the high-risk category do not have serious problems with AOD? Assuming that AOD use is potentially a problem for all adolescents, what are the differences between high-risk youths who never go beyond casual experimentation and mature out of use and those who become chemically dependent?

3. Research is needed to improve screening, assessment, and decision making for children and families affected by chemical dependency who are in the child welfare system.

There are a number of questions about the range of activities in which the child welfare system engages.

Referral to Child Welfare

When should parental chemical involvement trigger a referral to children's protective services? What discrepancies related to race or culture exist in the referral rates to child welfare? How do families with AOD problems get referred to child protective services? What is the disposition of these cases? How have dispositions varied with the parent's level and duration of drug use and drug of choice? Why are chemically involved African American women more likely than their Caucasian peers to be referred to child welfare for child protective service investigations? Is this discrepancy in referral rates due to institutional racism? Are other factors at work?

Placement Decisions

To meet the unique needs of infants and toddlers, we must have empirical data to improve outcome assessment and an objective analysis of intervention options and placement choices for infants and young children who were born AOD exposed. Research must also examine the degree to which pre- and postnatal environments exacerbate or alleviate problems posed by exposure.

What is the appropriate framework for placement decisions? What characteristics allow some chemically dependent parents to assure the safety and well-being of their children? What support services are needed to improve child welfare's ability to prevent inappropriate placements and improve the prospects for reunification?

Reunification Decisions

At what point in recovery is a chemically dependent parent capable of resuming parenting of a child? What factors other than the cessation of problem AOD use are barriers to reunification? Does abstinence improve the likelihood that the child will not return to foster care? Does abstinence correlate with reduced domestic violence? How do we explain the fact that minority children and children of substance abusers are less likely to be reunited with their parents? What are the factors that contribute to this outcome? If children are not reunited within a short period of time after placement, they are likely to remain in care for a prolonged time. This is particularly true when they are the children of substance abusers. What are the factors that account for this situation?

Risk Assessment

The AOD field has developed a number of tools for accurately assessing the severity of an individual's AOD involvement. Likewise, there are reliable, fully-tested child welfare assessment instruments designed to assess the risk of harm to a child. What is needed is an instrument that measures the degree and type of chemical abuse and the impact on parenting behaviors and resulting risks to the child. It is generally believed that there are inherent racial or cultural biases in most risk instruments currently being used. Research is needed to identify such biases and develop culturally sensitive protocols that are effective in assessing risk to the child, parental capacity to nurture, and level of impairment due to AOD use.

Effectiveness in Preserving Families

Another area in which research is needed is the effect of various support services, especially early intervention substance abuse services, on the ability of the child welfare system to preserve or reunite families and to identify appropriate child welfare interventions for different populations. Available data is primarily anecdotal at this point.

4. Research is needed to develop and evaluate model collaborative child welfare and alcohol and other drug treatment approaches for children, adolescents, and families in the child welfare system.

Researchers have already demonstrated to some degree that certain treatment approaches and AOD programs may be effective in promoting recovery. The factors essential for improving treatment outcome, however, have not been fully identified. Furthermore, there has been no attempt to evaluate the effectiveness of combining specific child welfare supports or services with specific AOD treatment models for different populations served by the child welfare system.

Even less is known about the design of culturally responsive programs for diverse clients. Do certain approaches enjoy cross-cultural success? What is and should be different? These issues are beginning to receive some attention. The Office for Treatment Improvement under the Alcohol, Drug Abuse and Mental Health Administration has recently begun to concentrate on these issues in relation to drug treatment. The child welfare system must also critically examine current practices and services to determine if they are responsive to the needs of diverse cultural populations and to identify and eliminate cultural biases wherever they exist.

Endnotes

1. Office of National Drug Control Policy, Executive Office of the President, National Drug Control Strategy, February 1992.

2. National Drug Control Strategy 1992, 2.

3. National Drug Control Strategy 1992, 2.

4. Tatara, T., "Children of Substance Abusing and Alcoholic Parents in Public Child Welfare," Submitted to the American Enterprise Institute by the American Public Welfare Association, 1990.

5. Complete results of the CWLA Survey of Alcohol and Other Drugs are available. Contact Patrick Curtis, Director of Research, CWLA, 440 First Street, NW, Suite 310, Washington, DC 20001–2085.

Appendix A

The North American Commission on Chemical Dependency and Child Welfare

Chair

Richard L. Jones, Ph.D.
President/CEO
Center for Human Services
Cleveland, OH

Staff Director

Charlotte McCullough
Director
Chemical Dependency Initiative
CWLA
Washington, DC

Executive Committee

Joseph Altheimer, Co-Chair
Practice/Training Subcommittee
Executive Director
Institute for Families and
    Children
New York, NY

Sheila Anderson, Co-Chair
Policy Subcommittee
Director of Residential Shelter
    Care
Children's Institute International
Los Angeles, CA

Peter Bell*
Special Advisor to the
  Commission
Minneapolis, MN

Sheryl Brissett-Chapman, Ed.D.
Chair, Research Subcommittee
Executive Director
Baptist Home for Children
Bethesda, MD

Joseph Borgo*
Program Consultant
Outreach Program
New York, NY

Ina Denton*
Program Director
Central Baptist Family Services
Chicago, IL

Lee Dogoloff, Co-Chair
Practice/Training Subcommittee
Executive Director
American Council for Drug
  Education
Rockville, MD

Elaine Johnson, Ph.D., Co-Chair
Program Subcommittee
Acting Administrator
Alcohol, Drug Abuse and
  Mental Health Administration
Rockville, MD

Ivory Johnson, Co-Chair
Program Subcommittee
Deputy Director
San Diego Department of
  Social Services
San Diego, CA

J. Lawrence Mendoza, Co-Chair
Policy Subcommittee
Program Evaluation Specialist
Metro-Dade Office of Substance
  Abuse Control
Miami, FL

Don Pranger*
Executive Director
Child and Family Services
Muskegon, MI

Stephen Torkelson, D.S.W.*
Consultant
New York, NY

Commission Members

Essa Abed
Director
Graham-Windham
Brooklyn, NY

---

* Members of the Commission who were also members of the 1989-90 CWLA
  Chemical Dependency Steering Committee

José Alfaro
Director of Personnel Training
   and Research
The Children's Aid Society
New York, NY

Deirdre Barrett
Executive Assistant
New York City Department
   of Health
Correctional Health Services
Brooklyn, NY

Loretta Butehorn, Ph.D.
Psychologist
Consultant
Boston, MA

John Calhoun
Executive Director
National Crime Prevention
   Council
Washington, DC

Diane Canova
Executive Director
Therapeutic Communities of
   America
Arlington, VA

Wendy Chavkin, M.D., M.P.H.
Senior Research Associate
Beth Israel Medical Center
Associate Professor
Columbia University School of
   Public Health
New York, NY

Gay M. Chisum, R.N.
Director
Perinatal Addictions Consultants
Chicago, IL

Shirley Coletti
Executive Director
Operation PAR
St. Petersburg, FL

Philip Coltoff
Executive Director
The Children's Aid Society
New York, NY

Ruth B. Davis, Ph.D.
Director
CASPAR Alcohol and Drug
   Education Program
Board of Directors, NACOA
Somerville, MA

Sherry Deren, Ph.D.
Principal Investigator
Narcotic and Drug Research, Inc.
New York, NY

The Hon. Christopher Dodd
   (D-CT)
United States Senate
Washington, DC
Patty Cole, Staff Person

Jerome Doyle
President/CEO
Eastfield Ning Quong
Campbell, CA

Margaret Dugan
Consultant
Dana Point, CA

Maureen Duffy
Service Director
Children's Aid Society of
   Metropolitan Toronto
Toronto, Canada

Abigail English, J.D.
Project Director
Adolescent Health Care Project
National Center for Youth Law
San Francisco, CA

Jim Fannin
Consultant
Strouse, Fannin & Associates, Inc.
Tallahassee, FL

Bracha Graber
Executive Assistant to the
   Executive Deputy Commissioner
Child Welfare Administration
New York, NY

Neal Halfon, M.D., M.P.H.
Associate Professor of Pediatrics
School of Public Health
School of Medicine, UCLA
Los Angeles, CA

Robert Horowitz
Associate Director for Child
   Advocacy
American Bar Association
Washington, DC

Judy Howard, M.D.
Professor of Clinical Pediatrics
Department of Pediatrics, UCLA
Los Angeles, CA

Della Hughes
Executive Director
National Network of Runaway
   Youth
Washington, DC

Beverly Jones
Senior Analyst
Center for Study of Social Policy
Washington, DC

The Hon. Joseph P. Kennedy
   (D-MA)
U.S. House of Representatives
Washington, DC
Mary Takach, Staff Person

Mary Jane Link
Executive Director
Task Force on Permanency
   Planning for Foster Children
Rochester, NY

Christine Lubinski
DC Representative
National Council on Alcoholism
   and Drug Dependency
Washington, DC

Allison Metcalf
Director of Grants and Special
  Projects
Brightside, Inc.
West Springfield, MA

Lou Nayman
Field Director
American Federation of Teachers
Washington, DC

The Hon. Major Owens (D-NY)
U.S. House of Representatives
Washington, DC

Leslie Parker
Budget Manager
Human Resources Administration
Office of Budget
New York, NY

Margaret Peak-Raymond
Executive Director
Minnesota Indian Women's
  Resource Center
Minneapolis, MN

David Pines, M.Ed.
Executive Director
New Futures—A Foundation
  for Today
Silver Spring, MD

Edward Schor, M.D.
Director of Functional Outcomes
New England Medical Center
  Hospital
Boston, MA

Toni Shamplain
President
Shamplain & Associates, Inc.
Daytona Beach, FL

Debby Shore
Executive Director
Sasha Bruce Youthworks
Washington, DC

Julius Simmons
Director
Cleveland Day Treatment
Beech Brook
Pepper Pike, OH

Reed Tuckson, M.D., M.P.H.
President
Drew University of Medicine
  and Science
Los Angeles, CA
(Special Advisor to the
  Commission)

Rita Watson
Family, Business Policy
  Consultant
Advisory Board Chair
The Mothers' Project
Yale/APT Foundation
New Haven, CT

Davene White
Neonatal Technical Coordinator
Howard University Hospital
Department of Pediatrics and
  Child Health
Washington, DC

Sis Wenger
President
National Association for
 Children of Alcoholics
Rockville, MD

Ilene Wilets, Ph.D.
Biomedical Statistician
Beth Israel Medical Center
Chemical Dependency Institute
New York, NY

Margaret Young, Ph.D.
Vice President
Young and Associates
Wichita, KS

Joan Levy Zlotnick
Staff Director
Commission on Families
National Association of Social
 Workers
Washington, DC

Technical Consultants

Laura Feig
Program Analyst
U.S. Department of Health
 and Human Services
Office of the Assistant Secretary
 for Planning and Evaluation
Washington, DC

Janet Hartnett
Deputy Director
Office of Policy and Legislation
Administration for Children
 and Families
Washington, DC

Coryl LaRue Jones, Ph.D.
Project Officer
ERB, DEPR
National Institute on Drug Abuse
Rockville, MD

Elizabeth Rahdert, Ph.D.
Research Psychologist
National Institute on Drug Abuse
Treatment Research Branch
Rockville, MD

CWLA Staff

Madelyn DeWoody
Liz Loden
Patrick Curtis
Maureen Leighton
Meredith Moss

Appendix B

Federal Programs Currently Addressing Chemical Dependency in Families*

PROGRAMS

Alcohol, Drug Abuse, and Mental Health Administration, Office for Substance Abuse Prevention (OSAP)

Pregnant and Postpartum Women and Their Infants Demonstration Grant Program

This program provides grants to public and private profit and nonprofit entities to demonstrate model service delivery projects for substance-abusing pregnant and postpartum women and their infants. Projects focus on prevention, education, and treatment in community, inpatient, outpatient, and residential settings.

---

* Information and technical assistance in preparing this section was provided by the staff of the U.S. Department of Health and Human Services.

The initiative supports over 100 community-based programs that provide or coordinate a comprehensive service delivery approach, as well as educational activities to prevent alcohol and other drug use during pregnancy and among women of childbearing age.

National Resource Center for the Prevention of Perinatal Alcohol and Other Drug Abuse

This national center, funded by OSAP, is intended as the country's focal point for policy, research, information/referral, training, service design, technical assistance, and evaluation of programs targeting chemically dependent pregnant and postpartum women and their children. The center will develop and disseminate promising prevention, treatment, and rehabilitation practices, while mobilizing communities and the nation to address the problems and negative health consequences of maternal drug use. The goal of this effort is to design a national center that can stimulate effective policies and practices for preventing and addressing maternal drug use and its consequences for children.

The center has four primary objectives:

1. To develop a national network of experts and practitioners who will provide information about program strategies so that innovative models can be rapidly shared throughout the prevention and treatment field.

2. To develop a system for the review and evaluation of policy, training, research, and service delivery strategies relevant to prevention, treatment, and rehabilitation for AOD-involved pregnant and postpartum women and their children.

3. To provide concentrated training for interdisciplinary teams to target community-wide changes in AOD prevention, treatment, and rehabilitation for pregnant and postpartum women and their children, as well as for groups of people who specialize in subareas of this field.

4. To establish a reliable system for acquiring national

baseline data to monitor progress made, as well as prepare a national report covering major aspects of this problem.

National Clearinghouse for Alcohol and Drug Information (NCADI)

NCADI has operated since 1987 as the central point within the federal government for the collection and dissemination of current print and audiovisual materials about alcohol and other drugs. NCADI has undertaken a number of activities relating to drug-dependent women and their infants, such as disseminating a special media kit for print and broadcast representatives that includes the latest scientific facts about alcohol and other drug use during pregnancy, examples of available public education materials, and resource lists. NCADI also regularly provides technical assistance and mailing support to the Healthy Mothers, Healthy Babies Coalition to launch a media campaign in conjunction with the National Alcohol- and Drug-Related Birth Defects Awareness Week.

Community Partnership Program

The Community Partnership Program provides grants for the purpose of creating and implementing comprehensive prevention programs. Approximately 200 grants were awarded in FY91. In FY92, the program will begin to target communities that have rates of alcohol and other drug use higher than the national average. The success of the year's activities will depend on rigorous conceptualization, design, implementation, and evaluation of the partnership and the prevention activities.

Conference Support

OSAP provides financial support for a variety of conferences each year that disseminate information on substance abuse to clinical and professional audiences. Several of the events have directly or indirectly related to substance-abusing pregnant and postpartum women and their children. A national conference on perinatal addiction is planned for July 1992.

National Institute on Drug Abuse (NIDA)

NIDA Maternal Drug Abuse Research Grants and Research Demonstration Grants

Research on maternal drug abuse and its effects on fetal and infant development is a top research priority of the National Institute on Drug Abuse. Its research program on the effects of maternal drug use seeks to identify the risks to the mother and child both before and during pregnancy; to develop better treatment programs for pregnant women; to develop new drug abuse treatment medications that will not cross the placenta and either not affect, or have minimal effects on the fetus; to develop ways of treating drug-exposed infants; and to develop better programs to encourage women to abstain from drug use.

AIDS Comprehensive Outreach Demonstration Project

These demonstration projects evaluate the efficiency of alternative strategies for reaching IV drug users and their sexual partners and persuading them to enter treatment as an AIDS-prevention measure. They include several that specifically address pregnant women.

National Surveys

The NIDA National Health and Pregnancy Survey will provide national estimates of the prevalence of drug use in women delivering live infants in hospitals and the number of drug-exposed infants and the prevalence of drug abuse during pregnancy by race/ethnic group, geographical distribution, and metropolitan/nonmetropolitan area; and information to assess the relationships among drug use during pregnancy, low birthweight, and infant's length of hospital stay. Data will be available in 1992/1993.

The Household Survey on Drug Use gathers data on the prevalence of drug use. Questions include whether the respondents have children, the ages of the children, and whether the children are living in the household.

The National Drug and Alcoholism Treatment Unit Survey (NDATUS) collects facility-level data on all drug and alcohol treatment programs in the United States. Beginning in 1990, the survey included questions on policy with regard to admitting pregnant women to treatment programs and the number and type of pregnant women in treatment. These data are being analyzed.

The Drug Services Research Survey (DSRS) has gathered data from a national sample of 1,000 treatment programs and included questions on policy regarding treatment of pregnant women and pregnancy status of clients. Data analyses are continuing.

The National Maternal and Infant Health Survey, sponsored by the CDC/National Center for Health Statistics, included questions funded by NIDA on the use of tobacco, marijuana, and cocaine during pregnancy. Data are being analyzed for the prevalence of drug use during pregnancy and for the apparent effects on child development through two years of age.

The National Survey of Family Growth, sponsored by the CDC/National Center for Health Statistics, included questions sponsored by NIDA on the prevalence of tranquilizer, stimulant, sedative, cocaine, and marijuana use during the last pregnancy. These data were collected from approximately 10,000 women in their childbearing years and are being analyzed.

The National Longitudinal Survey of the Labor Market Experience of Youth, a survey of youths and young adults in the labor market conducted by the Department of Labor, included questions funded by NIDA on the frequency of marijuana and cocaine use during pregnancy by an estimated 1,400 women who have given birth since 1987. This cohort is being followed and information about child development is being gathered and analyzed.

NIDA Drug Abuse and AIDS Public Education Materials

This program provides specifically targeted radio and print materials aimed at IV drug users and their sexual partners. The materials deal with three closely-related HIV issues: sharing needles, sexual relations, and childbirth. Materials include a videotape, television and radio public service announcements, posters, and print ads on the theme of preventing the transmission of HIV during sex, pregnancy, and childbirth.

Drug Abuse Information and Treatment Referral Hotline

NIDA operates a telephone hotline that has answered 250,000 calls in its four years of operation. The hotline callers have received referrals to drug abuse treatment as well as information on cocaine, other drugs, and AIDS. Half of the callers are calling because they themselves have a drug abuse problem and many are women.

NIDA plans to provide additional training to hotline staff to address concerns around substance abuse and pregnancy. They are also expanding the range of materials available for dissemination to callers.

NIDA Media and Communications Activities

NIDA has developed materials on drug use and pregnancy that have been distributed widely to the media and the public. They also plan to develop new materials, which will promote the hotline for women, provide guidance to professionals on outcomes of new research, and develop media materials to present findings, educate practitioners, and inform the general public on this topic.

NIDA's six-year collaboration with the Media Partnership for a Drug-Free America has resulted in the development of a major anti-drug abuse public service advertising campaign which include PSAs on substance abuse during pregnancy.

Office for Treatment Improvement (OTI)

Alcohol, Drug Abuse and Mental Health Services Block Grant

These funds are passed to the states, which use the money to serve target populations and purposes. In FY86 Congress created a 5% set-aside within this block grant for women's alcohol and drug abuse services. The set-aside was raised to 10% in FY89 for alcohol and drug programs and services designed for women (especially pregnant women and women with dependent children) as well as for demonstrations of residential treatment services to pregnant women. States use the set-aside for a variety of services and activities, including outreach, treatment, prevention, and training.

Campus Treatment Project

Through cooperative agreements between states and OTI, a number of facilities have been established where several providers, sharing common resources, deliver residential treatment services for drug use in a single large operation. The goals of this project are: (1) to enhance treatment capacity; (2) to improve the quality of treatment, especially through the provision of primary medical care and HIV/AIDS testing, counseling, and prevention; and (3) to create a controlled environment for assessment and evaluation of the efficacy of different treatment approaches.

Target Cities Programs

This program provides financial and technical assistance to nine large urban areas with high drug abuse prevalence. Funds are used to establish central intake, assessment, and referral unit(s) to facilitate appropriate patient-treatment matching and to coordinate an array of addiction, primary health, social, and vocational and educational services.

Critical Populations Grant Program

This program funds treatment services directed toward particular populations at risk including adolescents, racial and ethnic minorities, and residents of public housing, among others. Critical program focus is on the enhancement of existing treatment programs to ensure that patients are offered comprehensive services.

Primary Care Provider/Substance Abuse Linkage Initiative (SALI)

This initiative is designed to strengthen the linkages between the primary health care and the alcohol, drug abuse, and mental health treatment systems and promote increased awareness of addiction among primary health care professionals.

Waiting Period Reduction Grant Program

This program provides funding to expand drug treatment capacity in areas where patient demand clearly exceeds availability of service. In recent years priority has been given to expanding treatment for pregnant and postpartum women.

Criminal Justice Grant Program

This program awards grants to improve drug abuse treatment programs in state or local correctional facilities. Programs have been established to provide treatment services for inmates, probationers, parolees and juveniles.

Administration for Children and Families

Foster Care and Adoption Assistance (Title IV-E)

This program provides federal reimbursement for foster care maintenance payments to AFDC-eligible children and adoption subsidies on behalf of AFDC- and SSI-eligible children with special needs.

Child Welfare Services (Title IV-B)

This formula grant program provides funds for states' child welfare services, matching state expenditures at a rate of 75% up to each state's allotted proportionate share of appropriations. Appropriate services are broadly defined, and may include, for instance, case management, respite care, and parenting education. States are reimbursed for services provided to all children.

Child Welfare Research and Demonstration

This program supports research and demonstration activities in the field of child welfare, particularly to address preventive and other specialized services, foster care, family reunification, and adoption.

Temporary Child Care for Children with Disabilities and Crisis Nurseries Program

This program provides respite care to abused, neglected, or seriously ill infants and children, many of whom are from drug-involved families.

Head Start Program

Head Start is a comprehensive child development program that served approximately 548,000 low-income preschool children in FY90. Head Start programs emphasize cognitive and language development, physical and mental health, social services, and parent involvement. At least 10% of enrollment opportunities are made available to children with disabilities.

Substance abuse is a growing problem among Head Start families. In FY90, 12 family service centers were funded to demonstrate effective ways to reduce and prevent substance abuse, improve literacy skills, and increase the employability of the families of Head Start participants. In addition, funds have been made available for staff training and development of curricula aimed at preventing substance abuse. In FY91,

$8 million was awarded to 39 current grantees to increase their capacity to address substance abuse issues, including grants to support specific collaborative efforts between Office of Treatment Improvement (OTI) Target Cities grantees and Head Start grantees.

Comprehensive Child Development Program

This program funds centers intended to provide intensive, comprehensive, integrated, and continuous supportive services for low-income infants, toddlers, and preschoolers; to enhance their intellectual, social, emotional, and physical development; and to help families achieve self-sufficiency. Most of the centers provide AOD treatment referrals as needed.

Abandoned Infants Assistance Program

These demonstration projects: (1) demonstrate how to prevent the abandonment of drug-affected infants and toddlers; (2) identify and address the social service needs of drug-exposed and HIV-positive infants and their families; and (3) reunify these children with their biological families, when possible, and/or place the children in foster care. Most of the projects provide needed social services to the families, recruit, train and retain foster parents, and operate residential programs for drug-exposed children and children with AIDS. Respite care programs have also been established and health and social service staff have been recruited and trained to work with families, foster families, and residential care providers.

National Center on Child Abuse and Neglect
State and Discretionary Grant Programs

The National Center administers four state grant programs and a discretionary grant program to help state and local agencies address problems of child abuse and neglect. The National Center also supports research, evaluation, technical assistance, and clearinghouse activities. A number of grants in recent years have concentrated on families with substance abuse problems.

Drug Abuse Prevention for Runaway and Homeless Youth

This discretionary grant program funds public and private nonprofit agencies to address the problem of drug abuse among runaway and homeless youth. Grants support direct service provision and the improvement of local service coordination, particularly in underserved areas and in underserved populations.

Emergency Child Abuse and Neglect Prevention Program

This program provides grants to improve the delivery of services to children whose parents are substance abusers. Projects may involve the hiring of additional personnel, improved training, expanded services, and the establishment or improvement of interagency coordination.

Social Services Block Grant (Title XX)

The Social Services Block Grant (SSBG) program is the major source of federal funding for social services programs in the states. States may use some portion of the funds to provide substance abuse services. Eleven states indicated in their FY90 SSBG plans that they were providing substance abuse services with these funds.

Study of the Impact on Service Delivery of Families with Substance Abuse Problems

In July of 1991, ACF began an extensive study of the short- and long-term impact of families with substance abuse problems or AIDS on service delivery within ACF programs.

Health Resources and Service Administration

Community and Migrant Health Center Program Substance Abuse Initiative

This initiative is intended to integrate the special service needs of substance abusers. Activities include direct service as well as training and curriculum development for service providers in the community and migrant health centers.

Community and Migrant Health Center Program and Comprehensive Perinatal Care Initiative

The Comprehensive Perinatal Care Program (CPCP) supports the provision of case-managed prenatal and pediatric services to high-risk women and infants in 300 community health centers.

Maternal and Child Health Block Grant (Title V)

Block Grants are awarded to state health agencies to:
- Assure access to quality maternal and child health services, especially for people with low incomes and those living in areas with limited availability of health services.

- Reduce infant mortality and the incidence of preventable diseases and handicapping conditions among children; reduce the need for inpatient and long-term services; increase the number of children appropriately immunized against diseases and the number of low-income children receiving health assessments and follow-up diagnostic and treatment services; and otherwise promote the health of mothers and children.

- Provide rehabilitation services for blind and disabled individuals under age 16 receiving benefits under Title XVI of the Social Security Act.

- Provide assistance to children who are in need of special health care services by:

  Launching efforts to locate such children;

  Assuring them medical, surgical, corrective and other support services and care; and

Assuring availability of facilities for diagnosis, hospitalization, and aftercare.

Pediatric AIDS Health Care Demonstration Grant Program

This program encourages the development of a network to
help support women and children with HIV/AIDS and to
prevent further transmission of the disease. Emphasis is on
case-managed ambulatory services that will reduce the amount
of time spent in hospitals.

Health Care Financing Administration

Medicaid

The Medicaid program is the nation's principal source of
funding of health care for the poor. Eligible individuals must
receive needed services, including inpatient and outpatient
hospital services and physician services, in federally qualified
health centers. Since the Omnibus Budget Reconciliation Act
of 1989, states are required to pay for any Medicaid service
discovered on EPSDT screening to be medically necessary to
"correct or ameliorate any physical and mental illness" in
eligible children up to 21 years of age.

While Medicaid does not generally pay for drug treatment
or psychiatric services in residential facilities of 16 or more
beds, other forms of drug treatment, as any other covered
service, can be provided to program participants. Drug treatment can also be provided, at state option, as a rehabilitative
service or in residential treatment centers of fewer than 17 beds.

Improving Access to Care for Pregnant Substance Abusers (Medicaid Demonstration)

Medicaid funds are being used to demonstrate different
approaches for providing improved access to health care for drug-
addicted pregnant women and their infants. Five state Medicaid

agencies (Maryland, Massachusetts, New York, South Carolina, and Washington) will receive funds over a period of 4.5 years.

The five states will be modifying services and/or reimbursement approaches under Medicaid. Services that are not currently available under state Medicaid plans will also be included in some of the demonstration sites (e.g., residential treatment services). Features common to the participating states include community outreach and case management for pregnant women, provider awareness training, and support services.

Extending Medicaid Coverage of Substance Abuse Treatment to Eligible Pregnant Women: Assessment of Issues and Costs

The purpose of this exploratory research project is to study Medicaid's coverage of substance abuse treatment programs and to assess the costs of expanding this treatment to pregnant women at risk of delivering substance-impaired infants. This project will use primarily data from surveys that have already been conducted and data from interviews with state officials working in the areas of Medicaid and substance abuse.

Office of the Secretary, Assistant Secretary for Planning and Evaluation (ASPE)

Policy Research Regarding Substance-Abusing Women and Their Children

During FY90 and FY91, ASPE conducted several policy-related studies regarding maternal substance abusers and their children. This research included efforts to identify and describe promising approaches to serving drug-exposed children and their families; to determine whether there are differences in the characteristics, needs, services, and outcomes between the children of substance abusers and other children in foster care; and to better describe the population and needs of mothers and their children receiving care from comprehensive drug treatment programs.

Current efforts include the joint development, with the U.S. Department of Education and several DHHS agencies, of technical assistance materials for preschools and elementary schools regarding the educational needs of drug-exposed children, and secondary analyses of a number of existing databases with information on substance abuse by women with children and treatment services for this population.

Office of the Inspector General

Related Studies on Drug-Exposed Infants

The Inspector General's office produced four related studies regarding drug-exposed children and the child welfare system. "Crack Babies" examines how crack babies are affecting the child welfare system in several major cities. "Crack Babies: Selected Model Practices" briefly describes a number of programs providing services to drug-exposed children and their families. "Boarder Babies" is an advisory report describing the extent of the boarder baby problem in several cities. Finally, a report discussing legal issues surrounding prenatal drug exposure entitled "Prenatal Substance Exposure Laws: Do They Make a Difference?" will be released in early 1992.

Social Security Administration

Supplemental Security Income Program (SSI)

This program, administered by the Social Security Administration, provides income support to elderly, blind, and disabled individuals in low-income families, in foster care, or in institutions. Nearly 400,000 recipients are children or youths.

Drug exposure, per se, does not qualify a child for benefits, but drug-exposed children could receive benefits if their particular disabilities and family income and resources fall within program guidelines.

CONTACTS

Administration for Children and Families (ACF)

Administration on Children, Youth and Families (ACYF)

Wade F. Horn, Ph.D.
Commissioner, Administration on Children, Youth
  and Families, ACF
(202) 245-0354

- Child Welfare Research and Demonstration

- Abandoned Infants Assistance Program

- Drug Abuse Prevention Program for Runaway and Homeless Youth

- Study of the Impact on Service Delivery of Families with Substance Abuse Problems

- Emergency Child Abuse and Neglect Prevention Program

- Child Welfare Services (Title IV-B)

- Foster Care and Adoption Assistance (Title IV-E)

- Temporary Child Care for Children with Disabilities and Crisis Nurseries Program

- National Center on Child Abuse and Neglect State and Discretionary Grant Programs

- Head Start Program

- Comprehensive Child Development Program

Office of Community Services

Frank Burns
(202) 245-2892
• Social Services Block Grant (Title XX)

Alcohol, Drug Abuse, and Mental Health Administration (ADAMHA)

National Institute on Drug Abuse (NIDA)

Loretta Finnegan, M.D.
Senior Advisor on Women's Issues, NIDA
(301) 443-2158

Elizabeth Rahdert, Ph.D., Research Psychologist
Division of Clinical Research
(301) 443-4060
• NIDA Maternal Drug Abuse Research and Research Demonstration Grants

Barry S. Brown, Ph.D.
Chief, Community Research Branch
Division of Applied Research
(301) 443-6720
• AIDS Comprehensive Outreach Demonstration Project

Ann Blanken
Deputy Director
Division of Epidemiology and Prevention Research
(301) 443-6504
• Surveys

Richard Sackett
Visual Information Specialist
Office of Policy and External Affairs
(301) 443-1124; and
National Clearinghouse for Alcohol and Drug Information
(301) 468-2600

NIDA Drug Abuse and AIDS Public Education Materials
NIDA Hotline
1-800-662-HELP
• Drug Abuse Information and Treatment Referral Hotline

Mona Brown
NIDA Press Officer
(301) 443-6425
• NIDA Media and Communications Activities

Office for Substance Abuse Prevention (OSAP)

Bernard R. McColgan
Director, Division of Demonstrations and Evaluation
(301) 443-9110
• Pregnant and Postpartum Women and Their Infants
  Demonstration Grant Program

• National Resource Center for the Prevention of Perinatal
  Alcohol and Other Drug Abuse

Robert Denniston, Director
Division of Communication Programs
(301) 443-0373; and
National Clearinghouse for Alcohol and Drug Information
(NCADI)
(301) 468-2600
Ruth Sanchez-Way, Ph.D.
Director, Division of Community Prevention and Training
(301) 443-9438
• Community Partnership Program

Office for Treatment Improvement (OTI)

Susan Becker
Division of State Assistance, OTI
Acting Director
(301) 443-4060
• Alcohol, Drug Abuse and Mental Health Services (ADMS)
  Block Grant

Jerome Jaffe, M.D.
Associate Director, Office for Treatment Improvement
Acting Chief, Community Assistance Branch
(301) 443-6549
• Campus Treatment Project

• Target Cities Programs

Nick Demos
Chief, Special Initiatives Branch
Office for Treatment Improvement
(301) 443-6533
• Critical Populations Grant Program

• Waiting Period Reduction Grant Program

• Criminal Justice Grant Program

Saul Levin, M.D.
Director, Substance Abuse Linkage Initiative
Office for Treatment Improvement
(301) 443-8160
• Primary Care Provider/Substance Abuse Linkage Initiative

• Health Care Financing Administration

Debbie Van Hoven
ORD/HCFA
(301) 966-6625
• Improving Access to Care for Pregnant Substance Abusers
(Medicaid Demonstration)

Marilyn B. Hirsch
Office of Research and Demonstration,
Medicaid Program Studies Branch
(301) 966-7712
• Extending Medicaid Coverage of Substance Abuse Treat-
ment to Eligible Pregnant Women:

• Assessment of Issues and Costs

Carla Bodaghi
OLP/HCFA
(202) 245-0036
• Medicaid

James Hadley
ORD/HCFA
(301) 966-6626
• Demonstration Projects to Study the Effect of Allowing
  States to Extend Medicaid to Pregnant Women and Chil-
  dren Not Otherwise Qualified to Receive Medicaid Benefits

Lenore Carlson
Director, Division of Disability Process Policy, OD
(301) 965-9068 (FTS 625-9068)
• Supplemental Security Income Program (SSI)

Health Resources and Service Administration

Bureau of Health Care Delivery and Assistance (BHCDA)

Joseph O'Neill, M.D.
Acting Chief, Program Development Branch, BHCDA
(301) 443-2512
• Community and Migrant Health Center Program
  Substance Abuse Initiative

James Gray
Acting Chief, Program Implementation Branch, BHCDA
(301) 443-2512
• Community and Migrant Health Center Program and
  Health Care for the Homeless Program

Beverly Wright
Program Implementation Branch, BHCDA
(301) 443-7587
• Community and Migrant Health Center Program and
  Comprehensive Perinatal Care Initiative

Maternal and Child Health Bureau (MCHB)

Brad Perry
Branch Chief, Systems Services Development and Information
(301) 443-3163
• Maternal and Child Health Block Grant (Title V)

Eamon McGee
Acting Director, Office of Programs Support, MCHB
(301) 443-2170
• Special Projects of Regional and National Significance
  (SPRANS)

Beth D. Roy
Health Resources and Service Administration
(301) 443-9051
• Pediatric AIDS Health Care Demonstration Grant Program

Office of Population Affairs (OASH)

Barbara Tassey, M.D.
Medical Officer
Office of Population Affairs
(202) 245-0151
• Training of Title X Clinic Staff

Office of the Secretary

Assistant Secretary for Planning and Evaluation (ASPE)

Laura Feig
Program Analyst, ASPE
(202) 245-1805
• Policy Research Regarding Substance Abusing Women and
  Their Children

Office of the Inspector General (OIG)

Alan Levine
Program Specialist,
Office of Evaluations and Inspections
(202) 619-3409
• Related Studies on Drug-Exposed Infants

Social Security Administration

Lenore Carlson
Director, Division of Disability Process Policy, OD
(301) 965-9068 (FTS 625-9068)
• Supplemental Security Income Program (SSI)

Appendix C

Content Outline for
Core AOD Training

The practice/training subcommittee of the Commission strongly supports AOD training for the child welfare field in order to increase knowledge and develop critically needed skills. The subcommittee defined three levels of training.

The core training, designed for all child welfare agencies, should include basic alcohol and drug information and skill building and should be incorporated into existing preservice and in-service training for all staff members, caregivers, and volunteers who are in direct contact with children and families. The second level of training should build upon the core training and increase skills in assessment, case planning, case management, and community collaboration for staff members with responsibility for these areas. The third level of training is designed for child welfare agencies that plan to offer direct treatment services.

Core AOD training should give participants opportunities to:

- Explore attitudes and values about alcohol and drug use and working with chemically involved families.

- Build an understanding of the psychological, physical, social, and familial dynamics of addiction.

- Explore the differences between use, abuse, and dependency, and the different consequences of each on individual and family functioning.

- Recognize and understand characteristic behaviors and beliefs of chemically involved individuals.

- Understand the differential effects of various drugs and alcohol, the pattern of polydrug use, and the meaning of basic terms in the AOD field (*dependency, tolerance, relapse, recovery, denial, enabling, co-dependent,* etc.)

- Describe current trends, especially as related to racial/cultural/gender issues.

- Understand the relationship between chemical abuse and child and family violence.

- Understand the various roles family members may assume in chemically involved families and the impact of chemical involvement on the family system.

- Understand and be able to respond to the unique issues of children of substance abusers.

- Understand the different models and methods of prevention, intervention, treatment, and relapse prevention.

- Understand the nature of recovery and the need for ongoing supports and aftercare services.

The second level of training is designed to assist child- and family-serving agencies in better preventing and identifying alcohol or drug problems, and in making more appropriate referrals for treatment services. This training should be provided to all staff members who are directly responsible for assessing child or family strengths and needs and to staff members and caregivers who are working directly with families who are alcohol or drug involved.

Second-level training should provide participants with the knowledge and skills to:

- Develop and deliver AOD education and prevention information to the children and families served.

- Identify and access community resources related to AOD prevention.

- Understand and recognize the concrete indicators of an AOD problem.

- Accurately assess AOD problems at the time of intake and throughout the process of working with the child and family.

- Understand and be able to accurately assess risk and safety factors for children living with chemically involved families.

- Understand the appropriate usage and limitations of AOD toxicology screens.

- Effectively communicate about AOD problems with a child or family who is AOD involved.

- Identify and collaborate with community AOD treatment providers.

- Understand the benefits of community partnerships and the basics of interagency case coordination and case management.

- Recognize the different roles and goals of different community agencies.

- Develop strategies for team building and enhancing interagency cooperation.

- Identify barriers and gaps in the provision of services to chemically involved children, youths, and parents.

- Develop mechanisms for referrals to community AOD service providers.

- Identify and respond to the unique practice issues related to serving chemically involved families.

- Employ strategies for engaging nonparticipating agency members.

- Understand the importance of advocacy in promoting the full array of needed AOD services.

The third level of training is appropriate for agencies directly treating AOD problems in the children and families they serve. All staff in such agencies should be well trained and qualified to intervene with chemically involved individuals. Programs should be planned and supervised by individuals with strong AOD academic backgrounds and appropriate experience. In addition to assuring that staff members understand chemical dependency, the theories of addiction, various treatment approaches, and the advantages and disadvantages of various treatment models, training should also build an understanding of the importance of:

- Addressing racial, cultural, and gender issues.

- Placing chemical dependency in the context of an individual's overall strengths and needs.

- Involving family members in the treatment and recovery process.

- Using peer-based models, especially for adolescents.

- Incorporating relapse prevention as a central component of treatment.

The Child Welfare League of America (CWLA) has developed a comprehensive core AOD curriculum for child welfare providers. CWLA is prepared to provide technical assistance and consultation, in addition to training, to assist agencies in adapting policies and programs to better serve chemically involved children, adolescents, and families.